M000032759

Loving Neighbors
Far and Near

Loving Neighbors Far and Near

U.S. Lutherans Respond to a Hungry World

by Charles P. Lutz

Augsburg
Minneapolis

LOVING NEIGHBORS FAR AND NEAR
U.S. Lutherans Respond to a Hungry World

Copyright © 1994 Augsburg Fortress. All rights reserved. Except for brief quotations in critical articles or reviews, no part of this book may be reproduced in any manner without prior written permission from the publisher. Write to: Permissions, Augsburg Fortress, 426 S. Fifth St., Box 1209, Minneapolis, MN 55440.

Scripture quotations unless otherwise noted are from New Revised Standard Version Bible, copyright 1989 Division of Christian Education of the National Council of the Churches of Christ in the United States of America. Used by permission. Scripture quotations marked RSV are from Revised Standard Version of the Bible, copyright © 1946-71 Division of Christian Education, National Council of Churches. Used by permission. Scripture quotations marked NIV are from The Holy Bible, New International Version®. Copyright © 1973, 1978, 1984 International Bible Society. Used by permission of Zondervan Publishing House. All rights reserved. The "NIV" and "New International Version" trademarks are registered in the United States Patent and Trademark Office by International Bible Society. Use of either trademark requires the permission of International Bible Society.

Cover and inside design: Evans McCormick Creative
Cover photos: Frank Conlon/Wet feeding in Mogadishu, Somalia;
Joe Crachiola/Scene in a U.S. city.

Library of Congress Cataloging-in-Publication Data

Lutz, Charles P.
   Loving neighbors far and near : U.S. Lutherans respond to a
   hungry   world / by Charles P. Lutz.
      p.   cm.
   Includes bibliographical references and index.
   ISBN 0-8066-2761-1 (alk. paper)
      1. Lutheran Church—United States—Charities.   2. Evangelical
   Lutheran Church in America—Charities.   3. Lutheran Church–
   Missouri Synod—Charities.   4. Hunger—Religious aspects—
   Lutheran Church.   5. Poverty—Religious aspects—Lutheran
   Church.   6. Sociology, Christian (Lutheran)   I. Title.
   BX8074.B4L86   1994
   261.8'32—dc20   94-24888
                                                                     CIP

The paper used in this publication meets the minimum requirements of American National Standard for Information Sciences—Permanence of Paper for Printed Library Materials, ANSI Z329.48-1984. ∞™

Manufactured in the U.S.A.   AF 10-27611

98   97   96   95   94   1   2   3   4   5   6   7   8   9   10

CONTENTS

A MINISTRY CALLED "HUNGER"

- In the Peruvian village of Collini, high in the Andes, Jorge does not want to be forced off the land where he and his Aymara Indian ancestors have raised their own food for centuries. He and his neighbors seek and receive help for soil terracing and water supply through an agency made up of farmers' associations.

- Some 2,000 villages in drought-prone areas of India, which never before in their history had safe and dependable supplies of water, in a recent year received deep wells through a nationwide effort organized by the Churches' Auxiliary for Social Action. Through an interpreter, a village woman tells visitors, "The coming of this well has surely made my daily life a lot easier. It has also given me self-esteem, so that now I'm not afraid to talk with strangers like you."

> *The question of bread for myself may be a material one; the question of bread for my neighbor is always a deeply spiritual one.*
>
> —Nicolai Berdyaev
> (1874-1948)

- In southern Sudan, in the midst of a civil war, food is airlifted to the city of Juba. Hundreds of thousands of refugees are kept alive through an emergency feeding program operated by local Sudanese organizations.

- In the occupied West Bank, Palestinian young people receive training for work as welders, auto mechanics, carpenters, and electricians.

- In Brooklyn and the Bronx, New York City, federal money is secured to build housing for low-income people because of the effective work of an ecumenical coalition called "the Nehemiah Project."

- In San Diego, California, Lutheran Border Concerns Ministry mobilizes volunteers from area congregations to address human needs along the Mexican border. They work with food programs, home building, education, and medicine.

- In Marine on St. Croix, Minnesota, the Land Stewardship Project helps both urban and rural communities in the Midwest to understand the urgency of preserving farmland and creating a sustainable food system.

- In Harrisburg, Pennsylvania, the Lutheran Coalition on Public Policy helps secure adoption of a law which lets grocery stores give to food pantries food items that are outdated but still nutritious.

- In communities throughout the United States, local food pantries, month after month, receive gifts of food and cash from members of Lutheran congregations.

- In Lutheran congregations across the country, members write letters to their Congresspersons, urging expansion of the Women, Infants, Children (WIC) nutrition program, and make a worship offering of those letters as part of their citizenship response to God.

What's Going On Here?

What ties all these examples together is obvious. Every one is a response to hunger and poverty in our world. Each example is one small part of that which Lutheran people in the United States help to make possible. They do it through offering themselves—their money, their time, their citizenship, and their prayers—on behalf of neighbors both far and near.

All these examples, and many more, are stories of loving neighbors we may never see. The "we" refers to the great majority of U.S. Lutherans who are not poor and have seldom been truly hungry. Many of those not seen by us are invisible to us because they live halfway around the planet. Others, who are much closer, we may not see because we prefer not to go where they live: our inner cities, Indian reservations, isolated rural pockets.

It is true, as the writer of First John reminds us, that we cannot claim to love the unseen God and at the same time despise the brothers and sisters whom we see in need (1 John 4:20). It is also true that we are called to love many whom we do *not* see. We know about these sisters and brothers, we have heard of their need, and we demonstrate that the love of God dwells in us whenever we show love to them.

We Call It "Hunger"

In recent decades this ministry has borne the label "hunger." The word is frequently used as a generic term for a condition of physical want that is to be alleviated. In such usage, it means any material lack—not just of food but also of clothing, shelter, health care, and so on. Then, "hunger" is really a manifestation of extreme poverty.

"Hunger" is used throughout this book in that generic sense. Formally, however, the Lutheran Church–Missouri Synod (LCMS) uses "world relief program" and the Evangelical Lutheran Church in America (ELCA) uses "world hunger pro-gram" to cover these broad human-need categories.

In a way it is curious that hunger ministry has been named by the condition it seeks to alleviate. The churches have not, for example, put the name "war program" on their work in peace education. Yet, with a few exceptions ("Bread for the World" would be an example), it is the negative condition more than the positive objective that has seemed to communicate most powerfully.

And so we have this ministry of world relief/world hunger. It is a large enterprise in the two major U.S. Lutheran churches. For the LCMS and the ELCA (with its predecessor bodies), this organized work to alleviate hunger has been with us, in its pres-ent form, for roughly a quarter of a century.

In money resources alone, it has channeled through the two denominations, in less than 25 years, a quarter of a *billion*

dollars (an average of more than $10 million a year) to help
meet the physical needs of people. And, in a time when overall
resources available to national denominations are declining, the
trend line of giving by U.S. Lutherans for hunger alleviation
continues to be modestly upward. (See Appendix A for annual
income figures, 1970-93.) Further, it is estimated that congregations of these two Lutheran bodies give at least another $25
million annually to *local* charities, much of it for food and shelter assistance.

        And this money given by church members directly is not
the whole of it. Our hunger gifts have also made it possible to
procure, through advocacy with government agencies, additional
millions in tax dollars for alleviating hunger at home and
abroad. Because of the respect they have for the efficiency and
effectiveness of church-related efforts, local, state, and federal
governments consistently channel tax money on behalf of poor
and hungry people through them. Work funded in this way
ranges from local meals-on-wheels deliveries to sharing U.S.
government grain in the Horn of Africa.

Neighbors Far and Near

How did these efforts to relieve hunger in our world get started?
What is the current shape of their response to human need?
And what lies in the future for the churches' hunger ministries?

        This book is about such questions. It is about loving our
neighbor, nearby and faraway, whom we probably will never see.
It is about a ministry which is profoundly biblical in the way it
links a response to material need with a motivation that comes
from the heart of Christian faith. As the Russian philosopher-
theologian Nicolai Berdyaev wrote earlier in this century, people
of biblical faith cannot help but see that "the question of bread
for my neighbor is always a deeply spiritual one." Martin Luther
sounded a similar note:

> When faith leads to action in outward affairs, that which
> takes place is spiritual in the midst of the physical. Everything
> our bodies do, the external and the carnal, is called spiritual
> behavior, if God's word is added to it and it is done in faith.[1]

The Bible, of course, intertwines the material and the spiritual constantly, often through images of bread. The very first book of the Hebrew Scriptures is filled with stories of human interaction around food and famine (see Genesis 12:10; 25:29-34; 42:1-25). And that theme continues throughout the biblical record.

The prophetic writers instruct the faithful with such words as "pour yourself out for the hungry" (Isaiah 58:10 RSV). In the New Testament, Jesus cites the giving of food to hungry people as one sign of citizenship in God's kingdom (Matthew 25:31-46). The apostle Paul seeks financial gifts from the young churches to relieve the physical distress of "the saints at Jerusalem" (see Acts 11:29-30, Romans 15:25-27, 1 Corinthians 16:1-3, 2 Corinthians 8:1-15, Galatians 2:10). And the final book of the Christian Bible suggests that the problem of human hunger will ultimately disappear only when people are standing before the throne of God (Revelation 7:16).

About This Book

This book begins with the particular stories of seven creative congregations, local churches that have distinctive records of ministry among poor and hungry people. The next two chapters trace the development of hunger work over the past quarter century, from emergency activities to permanent ministries of U.S. Lutherans. Then, two chapters will look at continuing debates among us: one dealing with immediate relief versus long-term development, the other involving the politics of hunger. Chapter Six focuses on "people who are making a difference" in the battle against hunger. Finally, the reader will be asked to ponder the question "When will it all end?" as we peer into the probable futures of this ministry (Chapter Seven).

The book is intended not only for individual readers but also for use in parish study groups. A passage of Scripture and three additional items for group discussion follow each chapter. A study could be designed for seven sessions, one per chapter. Include the Introduction with Chapter One. (See Appendix E, Suggestions for Discussion Leaders.)

Readers should know that the author is not a disinterested observer regarding Lutheran hunger ministries of the past quarter century. My interest in the subject first took shape in the late

1960s and was sharpened during two years of staff work at the U.S. office of the World Council of Churches, 1969-71. From 1975 through 1980, I was the initial director of the American Lutheran Church (ALC) Hunger Program. That program was the responsibility of the ALC Office of Church in Society during the years I served as its executive director, 1981-87. Since 1986, I have been a member of the board of directors of Lutheran World Relief (LWR). In that role, I have been privileged to review LWR's work in three overseas settings during the past eight years: south Asia, the Middle East, and west Africa.

It should also be understood that all opinions not otherwise attributed are those of the author; they are not necessarily shared by LCMS World Relief or ELCA Hunger Program.

Acknowledgments

The author is grateful to a large number of people who have invested time and energy to help make the book come together. Foremost among them are Al Senske and Elaine Richter of LCMS World Relief and John L. Halvorson and Roger Livdahl of ELCA World Hunger; their initiative originally envisioned the book. These additional individuals made themselves available for personal contact with the author:

James Addington, John W. Bachman, Norman Barth, David Beckmann, Charles Bergstrom, Dorothy Borge, Stephen Bouman, L. David Brown, Carol Capps, Dolores Charlesworth, Jean Cordova, Vernon Cronmiller, Kathleen Daugherty, Kay Dowhower, Job Ebenezer, Brian Erickson, Elwyn Ewald, Dennis Frado, Jonathon Frerichs, Mildred Grady, Duane Hanson, Richard Hermstad, Dwayne Hoyer, George S. Johnson, David Keck, Julio Loza, Ed Markquart, Norma Marks, Robert Marshall, Norm McDonell, Larry Minear, Donald Nelsen, Mary Nelson, Marian Nickelson, Ken Peterson, David Preus, Alberto Rodriguez, Ted Schroeder, Rollin Shaffer, Arthur Simon, Joseph Sprunger, Robert Stackel, John Steinbruck, Shari Stelling, Arnold Tiemeyer, David Weeks, Glen Wheeler, Melvin Witt, Elisabeth Wittman, and Kathryn Wolford.

Finally, I wish to dedicate the book to my mother, Olga Cornelius Lutz, who of course told her own six offspring to "think about the world's starving children" as she reminded us to clean our plates. She also continues active today, at age 85, in the church's hunger ministry: quilting, giving, learning, advocating, and praying.

END NOTES

1. Quoted in *Luther on Vocation* by Gustaf Wingren (Philadelphia: Muhlenberg, 1957).

SEVEN CREATIVE CONGREGATIONS

It all starts in the congregations! When Lutherans in the United States seek to show love to neighbors anywhere in the world who are hungry and poor, it almost always begins with a local expression of their church. There are 17,000 of these local communities of the faithful in the Evangelical Lutheran Church in America (ELCA) and the Lutheran Church–Missouri Synod (LCMS). And no love-your-neighbor activity within them today is as fully established as that of helping the neighbor to find daily bread (i.e., to meet basic material needs).

> *Why is there such an abundance of social compassion in this congregation? I believe it is because Christ is walking in our midst.*
>
> —Keith Sanderson,
> Grace Lutheran,
> Des Moines, Washington

It is simply a fact: nothing our parishes do in direct social ministry comes even close to their collective activity in combating hunger. The consistency, the breadth, and the variety of hunger responses is impressive—whether one looks at preaching and teaching about hunger, at gifts of money and food to help people nearby and faraway, at forging personal links with people in very different economic circumstances, or at attention to shaping public policies that affect poor and hungry people.

Because the hunger response of U.S. Lutherans begins in their local churches, this book also begins exactly there. This first chapter profiles seven congregations which have been unusually creative in their antihunger work over a long period of time.

The number of potential candidates for inclusion was large. These seven are spotlighted because of their diversity of communities, their variety of membership sizes, and their geographic distribution. They are in large cities and small towns. In baptized membership, they range from 71 to 2,000. Three are in the East, two in the Midwest, and two in the West. The story of each is distinctive.

Kimball Memorial, Kannapolis, North Carolina

"We are not a congregation of rich folks," says Pastor David R. Keck of Kimball Memorial Lutheran Church in Kannapolis, North Carolina. "But we are generous." That statement is dramatically supported by Kimball's record of giving to hunger causes during the past 20 years. In gifts to the ELCA Hunger Appeal, this congregation in recent years has been averaging about $10 annually for each of its 760 baptized members. In addition, Kimball Church gives roughly another $8,000-$10,000 a year directly to social ministry efforts in its community, most of it targeted to poor people.

Kimball Memorial's hunger giving is likely so good because year-round education and action of many kinds surrounds it. Hunger is on the parish agenda all through the year. Each weekly bulletin and each monthly newsletter mentions hunger, including updates on giving for the year thus far.

"We probably have used every piece of material the Hunger Appeal of our church has provided," says Pastor Keck. "Our social ministry committee regularly shows videos on hunger, and we invite guest speakers to be with us. We recently had the chair of the ELCA task force on care of creation (Dr. Paul E. Lutz of Greensboro, North Carolina) talk with us about the church's new environment statement."

Envelopes for the Hunger Appeal are always available at Kimball Memorial. "We seldom have a Sunday without someone giving a hunger offering," Pastor Keck notes. "We once went something like 30 months without missing a Sunday!" Non-Sunday offerings during Christmas and Lent are divided between the ELCA Hunger Appeal and the local ecumenical ministry serving poor people (which Kimball helped to form). A freewill offering at the annual Shrove Tuesday pancake supper goes entirely to the Hunger Appeal.

Kimball Church usually has between 20 and 30 people participating in the local CROP (Christian Rural Overseas Program) hunger walk. The congregation also gives money and person power to Meals on Wheels, an area Habitat for Humanity project, and a local food co-op. Refugee sponsorship (Laotian and Vietnamese people) has been part of the parish program as well.

"One area where we're weak is in advocacy," says Pastor Keck. "We are a Bread for the World covenant church and give an annual $500 grant. A few of us write letters to our members of Congress, but we haven't promoted this as we should have."

A congregation of the former Lutheran Church in America (LCA), Kimball Memorial was organized in 1914. The textile industry historically has been the heart of the economy in Kannapolis, a city of about 36,000 people. "The congregation has no doctors, only two lawyers, but lots and lots of blue-collar workers," says Pastor Keck. "Many of our folks traditionally have been associated with towel and sheet manufacturing at Fieldcrest-Cannon Mills."

The congregation does not neglect other causes beyond the parish. It meets its ELCA apportionment in full, assists a Mission Partner congregation, provides partial support for a missionary in Japan, and recently raised more than $30,000 in a special appeal for Lenoir-Rhyne College, a nearby ELCA school. Indeed, about half of all church dollars given by Kimball members are put to work in ministries outside the parish.

"Our people have a pretty healthy attitude about sharing," Pastor Keck observes. "In the early eighties, a bequest launched a memorial fund, which has grown to more than $100,000. The congregation decided early to spend only the interest and to give every bit of that to causes outside the parish."

St. Matthew, Chicago

On Chicago's near west side is a congregation founded early in the 1870s by German immigrants. Today, the community served by St. Matthew is 85% Mexican-American. The parish's ministry is conducted in both Spanish and English.

This LCMS congregation is actively reaching out to the Hispanic people in its neighborhood. In years past, St. Matthew developed an Amnesty Center for the community. It helped to legalize 5,000 undocumented aliens and provided English and civics classes for some 2,500 students.

Since 1990 St. Matthew has operated a soup kitchen, *Comedor Popular*, which regularly serves about 300 unemployed and homeless persons. Organized by Mexican-American Lutherans at St. Matthew, during its first few years it operated with only local support. A grant from LCMS World Relief now assists the effort.

"We try to show a strong Lutheran presence in our community, with human care programs in family counseling, job training, food, clothing, and immigration services," says St. Matthew Pastor Julio Antonio Loza.

St. Matthew's caring is not limited to its immediate neighborhood. In the early 1990s, when a gas explosion in Guadalajara left many victims, St. Matthew collected and sent to that Mexican city 200 boxes of food, medicine, and clothing. The congregation also sent $6,000 in cash, which it had raised from church and community members.

"The problem of drugs and gangs in our community is not being addressed adequately by either secular or religious institutions," Pastor Loza says. "The temptation to give up or pull out is always present in the minds of those who struggle to live here. But our congregation is committed to stay and to minister as God gives us the opportunity to do so. We plan to continue a ministry of love and compassion among the needy families of Chicago."

St. Matthew is a small congregation, with about 180 baptized members. But its outreach is large. And its *Comedor Popular* is believed to be the only Lutheran-sponsored food kitchen serving hot meals anywhere in Chicago.

Grace, Des Moines, Washington

"This congregation's response to the hunger challenge comes from deep commitment to Christ and his compassion for the poor and hungry," says Norm McDonell, who chairs the world hunger committee at Grace Lutheran Church in Des Moines, Washington. "Instead of acting as burden, our commitment to combat hunger has seemed to be a major factor in the congregation's growth."

Grace Church, an ELCA congregation in a Puget Sound suburb near Seattle-Tacoma International Airport, decided at its annual meeting in January 1975 to raise $75,000 over a five-year period to combat world hunger. Grace intentionally combined education about hunger and its causes with an aggressive evangelism program. A core of dedicated lay leaders was to be trained for leading the parish in both objectives.

By January 1994, the beginning of its 20th year of anti-hunger commitment, Grace could point to these statistical developments:

• Baptized membership has grown from 785 to 1,500.

• Weekly worship attendance is an unusually high 50%.

• A goal of giving $1,000,000 to hunger ministries over 25 years (by the year 2000) was reached in 1993, seven years ahead of schedule; the great bulk of this giving went to the ELCA Hunger Appeal and Lutheran World Relief.

Other pieces of the story, while less quantifiable, are equally substantial. Grace has developed ongoing relationships with a sister church in Haiti, a medical mission in Jamaica, and (especially for its youth) an orphanage in Mexico. Among poor people locally, Grace works with homeless families in Seattle; with an Hispanic ministry (sponsored by the LCMS) in Toppenish, Washington; and with the Des Moines Food Bank.

Hunger education goes on continually. Individual memberships in Bread for the World are promoted. More than 100 Grace members have taken part in church-sponsored study trips to developing countries.

What makes it work at Grace? Norm McDonell cites several factors. "Strong pastoral leadership is a must," he says. Edward Markquart, who has been pastor of this former ALC (American Lutheran Church) parish since 1973, challenged the members as early as 1974 to become "a congregation of compassion," with antihunger work as the cornerstone. Biblical bread and justice themes are consistent in Pastor Markquart's preaching, and he has pioneered in creating parish curriculum on hunger for use in the larger church.

"We have also had strong lay commitment to the hunger issue," McDonell says, "and our hunger committee is one of the congregation council's standing committees. Including the poor and hungry always in the prayers of the church helps to keep the concern in the forefront."

Regarding funds, Grace insists that hunger gifts be over and above regular giving by members and never a scheduled benevolence budget item. At the same time, Grace believes that setting dollar goals has been helpful.

When Keith Sanderson, Grace's initial lay leader on hunger concerns, was recently asked why the congregation exhibited such an abundance of social compassion, he reflected for a moment and then replied, "I believe it is because Christ is walking in our midst."

"The key to it all is the power of the Holy Spirit working through the loving compassion of the laity," says Markquart. "When two or three key lay leaders agree on a needed ministry, and a larger group of eight or nine come together to work as a team—then this small core can influence the whole congregation. I also think Grace proves that evangelism and social ministry go together as two sides of the same love of Christ. If you want gospel wholeness, then it's going to be both/and."

St. Paul, Phoenix

A congregation of the LCMS on the west side of Arizona's capital city, St. Paul Lutheran Church has a vigorous social ministry program. While it generously provides funds for antihunger work overseas, the focus is on hunger in Phoenix and Arizona. Area hunger concerns comprise most of the work which is coordinated by the congregation's board of social ministry.

Much of the congregation's antihunger work happens through cooperation with other Christians. Lutheran Social Ministry of the Southwest (LSMS), an inter-Lutheran social service agency, receives about $4,000 annually from the congregation's budget. Statewide, LSMS helps poor and hungry people get needed assistance. It operates a food pantry in St. Paul's immediate neighborhood.

The 770-member St. Paul Church also joins with other Phoenix congregations in an ecumenical shelter and feeding program. St. Paul has been responsible the past four winters, with the help of LCMS World Relief domestic grants, for serving a meal every other Tuesday evening, December through March. The church is also a location for FoodShare, which offers groceries at low cost through a co-op buying effort.

"We are located in a very blue-collar area with lots of unemployed and underemployed people in this community," says Dolores Charlesworth, who chairs St. Paul's board of social ministry. "It's not always possible to get all our members to see the needs right around us, but we're working at it."

St. Paul Church regularly supports LCMS World Relief. Further, it recruits both walkers and pledgers for the annual community-wide CROP hunger walk. Money raised is channeled to Lutheran World Relief and to World Hunger Ecumenical Arizona Taskforce (WHEAT), the churches' agency for hunger advocacy in Arizona.

Charlesworth personally would like to have "more attention given to hunger and poverty in our churches' Sunday morning sermons. We could do a much better job of preparing pastors for a hurting world," she believes. "My hope is that some day our seminaries will address more deeply and more intentionally the all-encompassing message of the gospel."

St. Paul's, Waverly, Iowa

It was 1975 and Bread for the World, the fledgling Christian citizens movement against hunger, had announced its first nationwide Offering of Letters to members of Congress. The goal was to persuade Congress to adopt a Right-to-Food Resolution. The proposal would declare it to be "the sense of Congress" that every person on earth has a right to a nutritionally adequate diet because, without that, the right to life itself is denied. Co-sponsors were Sen. Mark Hatfield (R-OR) and Rep. Donald Fraser (D-MN). A young congressman (now U.S. senator), Charles Grassley (R-IA), had announced his opposition to the resolution.

Members and friends of Bread for the World who were Grassley constituents in Waverly, Iowa, invited him to meet with them at a local church. Following lengthy discussion of the resolution, Representative Grassley agreed to reconsider his position.

Soon after, Grassley did change his mind and became a vocal supporter of the resolution. The Waverly meeting was held at St. Paul's Lutheran Church, where many of those present were members.

At 2,000 baptized, St. Paul's is the largest congregation of the seven profiled in this chapter. Yet, it is located in one of the smallest communities (Waverly has about 9,000 people) and among its members are quite a number of farm families. For two decades, this former ALC congregation has shown a broad commitment to many aspects of antihunger work, and always the public-policy focus has remained central. Says Glen T. Wheeler, a pastor at St. Paul's 1975 to 1994, "The catalyst for this was certainly Pastor Dave Brown, who came fresh from leading the Freedom from Hunger Foundation in Washington" (see Chapter Two). "He helped organize one of Bread for the World's first chapters, and it's still going."

Waverly is also the home of the ELCA's Wartburg College and both faculty and students have been active in the local Bread group. "Among the many college-related people who have led us on bread-and-justice matters were Bob and Polly Dell, Dorothy and Herman Diers, Erna Moehl, and Barb and Warren Zemke," Wheeler recalls.

St. Paul's also stresses direct human connection with people overseas. Fran and Howard Mueller, one of the congregation's farm couples, and Pastor Dennis and Karen Dickman helped organize several cultural-exchange visits to rural Mexico for Waverly and Iowa people, through the Lutheran Center in Mexico City. St. Paul's has supported many international students at Wartburg; often, ongoing projects in their home countries have resulted. St. Paul's also stays in touch, via annual exchanges, with people in Chicago's Cabrini-Green Housing, where Holy Family Lutheran Church has been served for 19 years by a son of St. Paul's, Pastor Chuck Infelt.

The congregation was an early supporter of both Operation Bootstrap Tanzania (now Africa) and of the Waverly-based Self-Help Foundation, which seeks to assist food production in developing countries through appropriate technology. Both Howard Mueller and Dave Brown have served on its board. The same two were key to planning and hosting a consultation of ALC farmers on hunger concerns in February 1975.

Its K-6 Christian day school has given St. Paul's young people a strong educational base on the hunger/faith connection, Wheeler believes. Also significant is the fact that many former members of St. Paul's are serving overseas in church or government assignments. But the largest single factor in setting the congregation on its present course seems to be the leadership of one pastor in the 1970s. "Dave Brown has been gone from the pastorate here since 1979," says Wheeler, "but he supplied the original vision for our hunger efforts and that vision continues."

Concordia, McKeesport, Pennsylvania

McKeesport, a part of the greater Pittsburgh metropolis, is a casualty of the U.S. steel industry's decline. Since the early 1980s, the entire Monongahela Valley has suffered severe economic distress. The choice for Concordia Evangelical Lutheran Church, says Pastor David L. Weeks, "was either to close or to take on a different attitude toward our ministry."

Founded in 1888, this LCMS congregation at its numerical peak in 1977 had a baptized membership of just under 200. In 1981, when U.S. Steel was closing mills that had long been the economic lifeblood of McKeesport, Concordia began a two-year study, seeking to understand what God now wanted the congregation to do.

The study resulted in major changes for Concordia. The congregation decided God was calling it to reach out to a hurting community. It adopted a new mission statement which includes both proclamation of the gospel and addressing people's needs in a holistic manner. Concordia, it says, intends to "be a haven of rest through the proclamation of the gospel . . . through word and deed to those spiritually and physically in need in the McKeesport area."

This understanding of mission has led Concordia to open its facilities in order to address community needs. Since 1983, the congregation has operated Sonshine Kitchen, an emergency food bank, and a clothing bank. Sonshine serves meals each Monday evening to about 100 people. Those same evenings, clothing is available at no charge. Monthly, it distributes 800 bags of food serving more than 2,400 people.

About half of the budget for these ministries is provided by the congregation, the rest coming mostly from LCMS World Relief and other LCMS sources.

All of this is managed by a congregation whose size has declined to 71 baptized members! "The price has been dear," says Pastor Weeks. "Some members who had been good supporters left because they did not agree with our new directions."

But, for those who remain at Concordia, there is solid commitment to the outreach ministry. "We believe that the ministry's growth is evidence that the Lord is blessing us greatly," says Pastor Weeks.

Luther Place, Washington, D.C.

At Thomas Circle in the nation's capital stands a statue of Martin Luther, facing toward the White House, just a few blocks to the southwest. Behind the Luther likeness looms the red sandstone structure of Luther Place Memorial Church. The congregation has been there since 1873.

Swirling around Luther Place Church is a collage of "the good, the bad, and the ugly," in the words of John Steinbruck, the congregation's pastor for the past two decades. Adjacent are the offices of major national institutions (e.g., National Geographic Society, National Rifle Association, *The Washington Post*), foreign embassies and tony restaurants, posh hotels and expensive parking lots. There are also the remains of charred and boarded-up buildings, and street people of many kinds.

In this setting, Luther Place Church carries out a diverse ministry. The theological motif for this ELCA congregation's neighborhood commitment is *hospitality*. As Pastor Steinbruck puts it:

> Jesus is the "Bread of Life" and worship is the hospitality meal (the Eucharist) where we are hosted by the Host of hosts. Then, as surrogate hosts, we widen the communion circle to become all-inclusive of God's humanity, with priority for those excluded from our national feast (orgy). These are they who are *not* invited to White House banquets.

For Luther Place Church, hospitality translates into a continuum of neighborhood ministries addressing both immediate and long-term needs of homeless persons, especially women. These ministries are concentrated in N Street Village, a city block of church-owned town houses just north of the White House.

Luther Place Night Shelter provides lodging and meals for homeless women. Bethany Women's Center offers day services to help women regain self-esteem. Harriet Tubman House accommodates women recovering from substance abuse. Sarah House residents are women who have completed a residential treatment program and are receiving life skills counseling.

Raoul Wallenberg House and Carol Holmes House provide permanent residence for formerly homeless women who have mental disabilities. Anna Center is a place of respite for homeless women who are recuperating from serious illness or surgery.

Volunteers from the community contribute more than 20,000 hours of service annually, to support N Street Village's professional staff. Nearly all funds required to operate Village programs come from private sources.

With 370 baptized members, this congregation also tends to national and global needs. It is active in advocacy work with public agencies and generous in support of the ELCA Hunger Appeal. In 1979 it launched Lutheran Volunteer Corps (LVC). Through LVC each year, some 70 full-time volunteers work with social service agencies in half a dozen metropolitan areas: Wilmington, Delaware; Baltimore; Chicago; Milwaukee; Minneapolis-St. Paul; and Washington, D.C. Luther Place Church gives LVC free office space and equipment. While LVC has a distinct national identity, it is fully a ministry of Luther Place.

"Our goal is to give birth to these ministries and then let them function as spin-offs," says Steinbruck. "We'd like to see that congregation-initiative model become far more prominent among Lutherans."

Above all, Luther Place Church wants to be a hospice, an oasis, a place of refuge, says Pastor Steinbruck, "from the harsh environment of our capital's asphalt desert. We seek to be a place where our itinerant Savior can be at home and welcome outcasts, embracing exiles, those urban nomads who wander through life 'restless until they find their rest' in Jesus, at his banquet."

For Discussion

(Include the Introduction as background material for discussion of this chapter.)

1. Read Isaiah 58:6-10. What is it saying to the people of God in your congregation today?

2. Form seven subgroups and ask each to analyze one of the congregations, seeking to discover what makes it work. Have the subgroups report briefly to the full group.

3. Grace Church in Des Moines, Washington, believes a strong, biblical congregation will reach out both with the verbal proclamation of the gospel (evangelism) and with deeds of love and compassion (social ministry). Many Christians and congregations, however, seem to struggle to keep social ministry and evangelism in balance, and end up emphasizing one over the other. Does your congregation try to keep the two in balance? Does it succeed?

4. Concordia Church in McKeesport, Pennsylvania, decided to ask what God was calling it to be and do. Has your congregation asked that question in recent years? If so, has asking it affected the direction of your mission? If not, what values might there be in such an inquiry by your congregation?

DISCOVERING THE OTHER WORLD

Sharing bread with the less fortunate neighbor has always been an expected behavior pattern for people of biblical faith. Throughout the centuries of Jewish and Christian history, giving to poor people has been viewed as an evidence of spiritual devotion, a way of showing our gratitude to a loving God. This writer has vivid childhood memories of how churches in small-town Iowa were behaving in the latter 1930s. They made emergency funds available to provide meals at local restaurants for destitute travelers, who seemed always to be single adult males. Those churches also prepared and delivered food baskets at holiday times to families living in poverty, and these seemed mostly to be headed by single adult females.

> *The hunger I saw in India—both urban and rural—was absolute and devastating. I had never seen anything like it. It was a life-changing experience.*
> *I knew I had to come home and do something.*
> —L. David Brown

"Thanks to Hitler"

The first organized national efforts by U.S. Lutherans to address the distress of people overseas were prompted by World War I. During and after that conflict, the LCMS created a General Relief Board to give special attention to Europe. And in early 1919, an appeal for international relief was launched by the National Lutheran Council (NLC), which represented most of the non-LCMS Lutherans. It also focused on war-created needs in Europe and came to be known as

"Lutheran World Service." Over the next decade, that appeal sent $8,000,000 and more than 3,000,000 pounds of clothing for European relief. In addition, more than $700,000 was gathered for assistance to distressed Lutheran missions in China, Japan, India, and Africa.

But a more direct forerunner of today's world relief/world hunger appeals is the response of U.S. Lutherans to World War II. On September 1, 1939, Adolf Hitler's army invaded Poland. Within weeks, the National Lutheran Council (NLC) issued an emergency request for $500,000 to the people of the eight member church bodies (basically the constituency which is today within the Evangelical Lutheran Church in America). The money was needed, said the NLC, to help Lutheran refugees in Europe[1] and to assist Lutheran missions around the world that were now cut off from the support of European churches.

Within a year, Hitler's expansion had occupied most of western Europe, and it was clear that Lutherans in North America and in neutral Sweden were the only Lutherans who would have the resources to address war-generated needs. In the fall of 1940, the National Lutheran Council (NLC) issued a second appeal for $500,000 and began using the name Lutheran World Action (LWA). Though initially seen as a short-term effort, LWA would continue for almost four decades. In 1951, the eight churches of the NLC stated officially that the work of LWA would be a permanent responsibility.

And so it was that Lutheran World Action became a central activity of the participating churches. Its slogan, "Love's Working Arm," and its symbol, a muscular forearm thrusting forth a cross, assumed high visibility among many U.S. Lutherans. It was often observed that Lutheran World Action was among the more positive consequences of Hitler's reign of terror.

Meanwhile, the LCMS in 1942 had established a National Advisory Emergency Planning Council to coordinate the response to war refugees carried out by the Synod's Lutheran Laymen's League, Walther League, Lutheran Women's Missionary League, and other Synod entities. In 1943, the Synod joined with the NLC to form a Lutheran Commission for Prisoners of War, which provided spiritual services to the nearly half a million war prisoners scattered throughout the U.S.

In 1946, LCMS members gave for war relief more than $2,500,000, not counting the aid sent directly by families of Synod to needy fellow Christians in Europe. The LCMS response to war-caused needs continued via the Synod's General Relief Board through the early 1950s. In 1953 LCMS changed its name to Board of World Relief, appointed the first full-time staff director, and resolved that the Board should "upon short notice, bring comfort and aid where needed, and give effective Christian witness through such aid."

In 38 Years: $130,000,000

When Lutheran World Action was phased out in 1977, it was essentially because the world relief/world hunger appeals had taken its place. Through its 38 years, LWA gathered some $130,000,000. From 1946 onward, annual goals were usually in the range of $3,000,000 to $5,000,000, and they were almost always met. By the early 1960s, when mergers had reduced the number of supporting churches to two (the American Lutheran Church and the Lutheran Church in America), LWA was incorporated into the regular budgets of those churches. After 1967, LWA was administered by the Lutheran World Federation's USA National Committee (later known as Lutheran World Ministries), which represented the same two churches, ALC and LCA. The Association of Evangelical Lutheran Churches, when it was formed in 1976, became a third partner.

While most of the LWA money was used for what today would be considered hunger-combating work, other causes also benefited. LWA at times supported, for example, cooperative mission work, younger overseas churches, and other international church activities, even pastoral services to U.S. military personnel. But it also gave major support to both Lutheran World Relief, organized by U.S. Lutheran churches in 1945, and to Lutheran World Federation, created by the global Lutheran family in 1947.

"In the very early years of LWA, the emphasis had to be on war-orphaned missions and ministries to U.S. personnel, and then war-devastated congregations," writes the Rev. Rollin G. Shaffer, an LWA staff person from 1948 to 1977. "Service to refugees was also a part of LWA from the very start. By the 1970s, when the churches began their hunger appeals, much of what

LWA supported was in the realm of meeting material needs of people, what we now define as antihunger work."

Next: Lutheran World Relief

Lutheran World Relief (LWR), when formed in the fall of 1945, was assumed to be another response to immediate need which would have a short life. It was initially a clothing appeal, to aid displaced persons in the aftermath of the war in Europe. Soon other forms of material aid were added, especially food and medicines. Help went to fourteen countries in Europe and eight in Asia in the immediate post-war years.

LWR was created initially by the eight churches of the National Lutheran Council. In 1953, the LCMS became an informal partner and two years later it joined as a full voting member of LWR. Essentially these same constituencies (the nearly 8,000,000 members of LCMS and ELCA) provide LWR's support today. (The 420,000-member Wisconsin Evangelical Lutheran Synod, while electing not to join as a participating church, has for years given an annual grant to LWR. A few individuals and congregations from smaller Lutheran bodies also contribute to LWR from time to time.)

LWR's attention shifted from World War II's aftermath to the developing nations of Asia, Africa, and Latin America, beginning in the mid-1950s. Today, its work is concentrated in those low-income regions of the planet, and its resources from the churches come entirely via the LCMS World Relief and ELCA World Hunger offerings (some individuals of both churches also contribute directly to LWR). In addition, it should be noted that, in years when there are major international emergencies, material aid resources channeled through LWR by the U.S. government may, in dollar value, far surpass all resources provided by the churches.

From the beginning, the churches have asked that LWR's work be outside the borders of the United States. While most of its focus initially was on aiding Lutherans and other Christians in Europe, LWR today is understood by its supporting churches to be their primary vehicle for material aid to suffering people anywhere overseas. Further, they want that help to go to people *without regard to their politics, religious faith, or ethnicity.* The sole question is whether such people have severe material need. Finally, the churches do not look to LWR for evangelistic work or for support to the Word and Sacrament ministries of overseas churches. Such activities the churches support through their own world mission boards.[2]

Lutheran World Federation

Two years after the formation of Lutheran World Relief, an international association of most Lutheran denominations was created in Lund, Sweden. The new Lutheran World Federation (LWF) gave immediate attention to helping war-devastated Lutheran churches, not only in Europe but also in such places as Japan, China, New Guinea, and Indonesia. In the late forties and early fifties, more than 90% of the money for such church-rebuilding came from Lutheran World Action in the U.S.

By the mid-fifties, Lutherans were using LWF for a purpose quite different from rebuilding churches. Its Department of World Service was becoming a major global player in addressing human needs, particularly refugee work. And now, almost none of the recipients were Lutherans; indeed, most were not Christians. By 1965, LWF World Service was operating in more than 30 countries on six continents. For years, it has been the world's largest Protestant agency for humanitarian assistance.

Some of the work of LWF World Service is short-term and transitory, such as emergency response to the needs of people uprooted by the Persian Gulf War in 1991. Many of its programs, though, tend to last for quite a while. Since the late forties, for example, LWF World Service has provided health care for Palestinians through Augusta Victoria Hospital in Jerusalem and through village clinics. For three decades it has been serving refugees from several east African nations in Tanzania (LWF in mid-1994 became the lead agency for aiding Rwandans who fled into Tanzania by the hundreds of thousands). For over two decades, it has operated a comprehensive rural development project in Bangladesh which dwarfs all other nongovernmental efforts in that Asian country.

At one time, U.S. Lutherans were the largest provider of resources to LWF World Service. But for the last three decades, U.S. contributions have been eclipsed by those from Scandinavian and German churches. Still, U.S. participation remains substantial. All of the ELCA money today is from world hunger gifts. Also receiving ELCA hunger money in recent years has been the LWF Department for Mission and Development. In 1993, the total of ELCA hunger dollars going to LWF was about $3,500,000.

LWF also receives a significant amount from LCMS World Relief, for support of both emergency activities and long-term development projects. Though LCMS is not a member church of LWF, in a typical 12-month period, about $100,000 in LCMS funds may go to work through LWF World Service.

By 1950: Vehicles in Place

Thus it was that, by the midpoint of the twentieth century, U.S. Lutherans had taken part in organizing several vehicles for responding to human needs around the planet. Lutheran World Relief and the agency that would later be known as Lutheran Immigration and Refugee Service were the direct creation of U.S. Lutherans. Before the 1940s ended, some U.S. Lutherans had joined with other U.S. Protestant and Orthodox churches to establish Church World Service, and with overseas Lutherans had formed Lutheran World Federation.

The partnership between Lutherans and Church World Service (CWS) is an interesting one. Because U.S. Lutherans have their own agency (LWR) for overseas development and relief ministry, they give relatively few dollar resources to CWS. Yet, the ELCA is a full participant in the agency. Further, as early as 1948 the LCMS was associated with the CWS program known as CROP (Christian Rural Overseas Program). Members of both churches across the country take part in annual CROP walks for hunger. And, through LWR, both churches are involved with the Office on Development Policy in Washington, D.C., which is operated jointly with CWS (see Chapter Five).

At their beginnings, financial support for these several agencies came from a variety of sources within the U.S. Lutheran churches. It would be another 20 years before permanent funding of them would shift primarily to avenues called "world hunger" and "world relief."

Changed by the 1960s

Today, we consider sermons and education sessions on hunger standard in parish life. Likewise taken for granted in many congregations are the year-around presence of world relief/world hunger offering envelopes, of reminders to bring items for the local food shelf, and perhaps of encouragement to let politicians know our attitudes about poverty and hunger. But it was not always so.

The biblical connections between loving our neighbor and daily bread are not new. Just as "the poor you will always have with you" (Matthew 26:11 NIV), so also God's people have had the biblical material on poverty and hunger for as long as we've had the Hebrew and Greek Scriptures. What is new in recent decades for U.S. Lutherans is our focused, coherent, and continuing attention to that part of biblical theology.

What happened to make this change? How did the concern for alleviating hunger become institutionalized in U.S. Lutheran life?

To seek some answers, one must look at that watershed decade in American society, the 1960s. It was a time of dramatic change in this nation's outlook on many things. Our culture and our politics were taking new directions. So were our ways of understanding Christian discipleship. It wasn't the gospel, God's eternal promise of love and salvation to humankind, that was changing. But our sense of what is a fitting *response* to the gospel—the ethics that should flow from the faith God has given us—on this we underwent a major shift. We began to see our neighbor's physical well-being as a priority on our neighbor-love agenda. We again looked seriously at the faith/deeds question posed by the Letter of James:

> What good is it, my brothers and sisters, if you say you have faith but do not have works? . . . If a brother or sister is naked and lacks daily food, and one of you says to them, "Go in peace; keep warm and eat your fill," and yet you do not supply their bodily needs, what is the good of that? (James 2:14-16).

And perhaps we rediscovered the same theme in Martin Luther's Large Catechism (Explanation to the Fifth Commandment): "If you see [people] suffer hunger and do not feed [them], you have let [them] starve. It will do you no good to plead that you did not contribute to [their] death by word or deed, for you have withheld your love from [them] and robbed

[them] of the service by which [their lives] might have
been saved."

In Our Public Life[3]

Early in the 1960s, a commitment to end poverty in the low-
income parts of the world was gathering momentum. Most of
the poorest countries were new nations, just emerging from
colonialism. The United Nations launched its first Development
Decade, President John F. Kennedy and the U.S. Congress created the Peace Corps, and the U.S. government also gave birth
to its Agency for International Development.

Further, President Kennedy helped to establish the American Freedom from Hunger Foundation (AFFHF), following the
lead of the U.N. Food and Agriculture Organization (FAO). FAO
had proposed a global movement of citizens called "Freedom
from Hunger/Action for Development." Its goals were to raise
public awareness about poverty, to collect money for grassroots
self-help projects, and to promote support for governmental
assistance to improve agriculture and rural development. This
international network's First World Food Congress was hosted in
the U.S. by the new AFFHF in 1963. Later in the decade,
AFFHF was pioneering educational and fund-raising activity
through "walks for development" in hundreds of local communities across the nation. Though it would be gone within a dozen
years, AFFHF's later life would have significant Lutheran connections (see "Youth Ministry's Cutting Edge," below).

Toward the end of the decade, civil war in Nigeria (the
Biafran revolt) captured major press attention. Concern for
starving Biafrans heightened worldwide awareness of hunger.

The image of poor and hungry people within the United
States was also coming into focus. Michael Harrington's 1962
book, *The Other America*, had massive impact on the awareness of
both the public and their political leaders. Church groups prepared study guides to it and many congregations held weeks-
long discussions. The new citizen awareness helped to create, in
the mid-1960s, the federal programs which came to be called the
"war on poverty." A number of these, including Headstart, the
Job Corps, and federal food programs, are still with us.

In the Churches

The decade of the sixties brought new attention to the poverty/
hunger concern also in the churches. Clearly, this attention par-
alleled public-sector activities. But not only that. In many
northern-world nations, including the United States, the
churches were discovering anew the world of the southern hemi-
sphere. And the churches' commitment to the South in key
respects led the way in stimulating and shaping a governmental
response.

For many U.S. Lutherans, the new factor was growing
exposure to southern-hemisphere realities, and that exposure
came primarily through the global church. L. David Brown, a
now-retired bishop of the former American Lutheran Church
and the Evangelical Lutheran Church in America, is a striking
example. In 1961, when Brown was youth director of the ALC,
his church named him a delegate to the World Council of
Churches Third Assembly in New Delhi, India.

"India was my first exposure to hunger," Brown recalls.
"Hunger—both urban and rural—that was absolute and devastating. I had never seen anything like it. It was a life-changing
experience for me. I knew I had to go home and do something."

Youth Ministry's Cutting Edge

Brown went home, back to his work and, for the next seven
years, those life-changing discoveries in India affected the youth
ministry of one major Lutheran denomination. He also recalls
that during the 1960s "the youth committees of both the
Lutheran World Federation and the World Council of Churches
provided a cutting edge for the churches on hunger."

Toward the end of the decade, Brown "had to get some
academic grounding in the issue, so I took some courses in agricultural economics at the University of Minnesota." In the
spring of 1969, this Midwest Lutheran pastor was called to
Washington, D.C., to lead the American Freedom from Hunger
Foundation as executive director.

"I'd been on its board since 1964 and it seemed to be the
ministry to which God was calling me" at that time, Brown says.
"The foundation was still connected to the federal government,
with loose ties to both State and Agriculture departments; they

gave us free office space and telephone service. But otherwise we raised our own funds." It was done chiefly through walks for development and "third-world shops," local outlets for selling crafts from developing countries. "The first AFFHF walks were in the Fargo-Moorhead area in 1964," Brown remembers. "Lutheran young people really took the lead."

Brown remained with AFFHF until the summer of 1973. (The organization folded a year or two thereafter, apparently because a young and brash staff leadership had lost touch with the foundation's constituency.)

First CROP Walk

Lutheran youth in North Dakota pioneered another hunger walk in this period. The first Church World Service/CROP Walk for Hunger was planned in Bismarck in 1969 as a joint effort of the Luther Leagues of the ALC Western and Eastern North Dakota districts. Brian L. Erickson, then president of the Eastern District League and a sophomore at Concordia College in Moorhead, Minnesota, was a prime youth organizer. Pastoral advisors were Milton Ost, now serving Grace Church in Albert Lea, Minnesota, and James Schoeld, currently pastor of Bethel Church, Seattle. Erickson, senior pastor of Peace Church in Fargo since 1991, still carries a vivid picture of the weekend:

> Our theme was "People Are Dying—and We Say We Care." Our keynoter was Dave Brown, who had just gone to the Freedom from Hunger Foundation in Washington. We wanted to do more than pass a hunger resolution, to find a way to make a difference on the issue. So we asked youth to bring money pledges from their home communities. We had about 1,000 people on the 10-mile walk south of Bismarck. In those days, large marches were being held for racial justice. We were marching for *economic* justice.

The hunger walk raised $23,000, of which $17,000 went to Church World Service/CROP and $6,000 to the ALC Crisis Fund, which had been created by the church's 1968 convention to respond to urban needs. "It was especially exciting for me to be able to deliver personally that $17,000 check to the CROP

office in Elkhart, Indiana," Erickson recalls. "When you see how
the CROP walks have become a national tradition in the 25
years since, I think it's one more example of how God takes our
loaves and fishes, and multiplies them again and again."

Young people in the LCMS were also taking initiatives for
hunger. They asked the Synod's 1969 convention, for example,
to declare a two-year moratorium on new building construction
within the church, devoting the resources saved to the alleviation of hunger. The convention declined that proposal, but
specifically thanked the youth for raising hunger awareness.

Hunger Becomes the Focus

The three major U.S. Lutheran churches had been addressing
world poverty together for the previous two decades, of course,
through Lutheran World Relief and Lutheran World Federation.[4] And the LCMS Board of World Relief had been in place
since 1953. Now, with the sixties ending, initiatives having specific "hunger" focus would be taken by Lutheran bodies. The
first such action came at the 1969 LCMS convention, July 11-18,
in Denver.

The convention instructed the Synod's Board of Directors
to appoint a committee to coordinate efforts in the LCMS "to
alleviate world hunger." The committee should "consult and
cooperate with other religious and secular organizations in
determining the most effective ways and means to meet the
need of hungry humanity." The convention also agreed to provide Synod funds to cover administrative costs of the Board of
World Relief, plus another $100,000 "to feed at least a few of
the hungry of this world now." It challenged Synod congregations and members:

- to give "sacrificially" and

- to write members of Congress and other government officials
  about the hunger concern and the need "to reassess our
  national values and priorities in order to deal more effectively
  with world hunger."

Delegates took these actions in the belief that "Christians,
set free from self-centeredness by the crucified and living Christ,

have the desire to meet their Lord's directive to 'feed the hungry.' "

The Commission on World Hunger, created because of the 1969 convention action, served in coordination of LCMS hunger concerns for the next six years. It worked closely with the LCMS Board of World Relief. In 1970 the World Relief office, which had been located in the Detroit area since 1953, moved to Synod headquarters in St. Louis so that coordination among all LCMS units would be more efficient. The Rev. Martin C. Poch was named executive director for the LCMS Board of World Relief.

LCA and ALC Responses

It would be a few more years (1974) before the other two major Lutheran bodies created official structures for hunger response. But they were not silent in the meantime. The Lutheran Church in America had addressed domestic hunger in "Poverty," a statement adopted in 1966 (Kansas City convention). Its 1970 Minneapolis convention statement, "World Community," gave strong endorsement to official development aid to low-income countries, especially through multilateral channels. It also called for just sharing of the resources of the seas with the world's poorest nations.

In the ALC, hunger was a major item at its 1968 convention (October 16-22, Omaha). There, as for the LCMS in 1969, youth had a big role. Gerald Glaser, first vice president of the Luther League, formally addressed the convention on hunger. Concern with poverty and racism in U.S. society, highlighted by major urban unrest, led to adoption of a churchwide response; it included a process for funding community-based projects (later named Development Assistance Program). President Fredrik A. Schiotz, while strongly endorsing the response to domestic turmoil, asked delegates not to overlook needs in the developing world. He specifically urged the ALC to protest a Congressional cut in U.S. foreign aid and to endorse a proposal from the 1968 Assembly of the World Council of Churches: that each developed nation give 1% of its gross national product as aid to the developing nations.

The convention did not act specifically on either of President Schiotz's suggestions. But it did adopt "Hunger in the

World" as a position paper of the church. The document ana-
lyzes hunger's causes and the strategies available for addressing
it. It calls on members to "support constructively helpful efforts
of both governmental and voluntary agencies to solve the world
hunger problem" and to respond to the needs of all people.

New Impetus in 1974
World hunger was a front-page story for most of 1974. There
were three major reasons:

● A lengthy drought in the Sahel region of Africa—from Sene-
gal to Ethiopia—had produced a crushing famine; the world's
media discovered it and decided to give it major attention.

● Low wheat harvests in the Soviet Union the previous fall led
that country into a massive purchase of grain on the world
market, reducing global stocks and driving up prices (for, as it
turned out, only a short time).

● The governments of the planet were getting ready for a
World Food Conference, called by the U.N. for that November in Rome.

World hunger was thus receiving coverage, day after day,
in the popular media. It all helped to make 1974 a watershed
year for church people in organizing against hunger. A new
Christian citizens group, Bread for the World (which had origi-
nated in a single congregation in lower Manhattan—see Chapter
Five), was going national. The mainline denominations formed
the Interreligious Task Force on U.S. Food Policy to work with
political power centers in Washington. The National Council of
Churches created a Working Group on Domestic Hunger and
Poverty.
And, early in 1975, Lutheran World Relief and Church
World Service jointly opened an office in Washington to focus
on federal policy.

Three Church Body Actions
Thus it was that 1974 became a time for the three major U.S.
Lutheran churches also to make specific responses.

- The LCMS Board for World Relief was in the midst of its first world hunger appeal. Already at its 1971 convention in Milwaukee, LCMS had asked its congregations to observe an annual World Relief/World Hunger Sunday. At its July 1973 New Orleans convention, the Synod had established a $1 million goal for addressing overseas hunger. It now contracted with Dr. William J. Danker, a professor at Concordia Seminary in St. Louis, to coordinate the hunger appeal.

- The Lutheran Church in America's 1974 convention at Baltimore established a world hunger appeal. Gifts were to be used for four purposes:

   1. Immediate relief of hunger;
   2. Development programs to deal with endemic need;
   3. Sensitizing the constituency as to the nature and extent of this crisis; and
   4. Support of governmental programs designed to deal with this crisis.

   The Baltimore LCA convention also endorsed "Toward the Development of a U.S. Food Policy," a statement issued earlier in the year by Lutheran World Relief.

- A majority of ALC district conventions in the spring of 1974 passed resolutions asking the national Church Council to create a hunger appeal; the effort had been orchestrated by the ALC Committee on Rural Ministries. In June, the Council did launch an emergency hunger appeal. The ALC met in convention four months later, in Detroit, under the theme "Ministering to a Hungry World." Featured guest was President Gerald R. Ford, who had come to his office only two months before, upon the resignation of President Richard Nixon. Ford struck a note of sacrifice as he told ALC delegates:

   I am hopeful that we will be able to continue America's humane tradition . . . and, as I have told the American people, sacrifices will be required. Our lifestyles to some extent must be adjusted if we are to remain a source of strength for all peoples.

The ALC created its own world hunger appeal at that October 1974 convention. In doing so, delegates expressed their "willingness to change our standard of living," specifically designated Thanksgiving as a proper time for ingathering of funds, and instructed the church's president to establish a Committee on World Hunger "to give leadership and direction" to the ALC's hunger response. The convention also voted to devote 50% of an expected excess in 1974 ALC benevolence receipts to world hunger.

Now all three major Lutheran churches had vehicles in place for an ongoing financial response to world poverty and hunger. As it turned out, some who supported the creation of those vehicles had not envisioned them as permanent fixtures. But, for more than two decades now, that is clearly what they have become. Exactly how these antihunger efforts grew into full parts of the churches' regular mission enterprise will be told in later chapters.

For Discussion

1. Read and discuss Psalm 9:18. What is it saying to the people of God in your congregation today?

2. What do you think of the long-term understanding that Lutheran World Relief limit its work to material assistance, leaving global evangelization and gospel proclamation to other arms of the church? Chapter One suggests it is an unbiblical separation for a congregation (see Discussion Item 3). Can you think of reasons why it might be appropriate for an agency like LWR?

3. For those who are old enough, share recollections you have from the turbulent 1960s. What do you believe is different now because of changes which started then?

4. Discuss the role of the media in putting hunger on our personal and church agendas. To what extent do the media—both secular and church—shape our responses to hunger? What are the pluses of media influence? The minuses?

END NOTES

1. Lutheran Refugee Service became part of the National Lutheran Council in 1939. Lutheran World Action was its primary church funder for many years. LCMS in 1954 became a partner in this work. Today, renamed Lutheran Immigration and Refugee Service, it continues as an independently incorporated joint agency of ELCA, LCMS, and the Latvian Evangelical Lutheran Church. ELCA funding is from both that church's benevolence budget and (since 1992) hunger funds. Its LCMS support comes from LCMS World Relief domestic funds. For the story of its first half century of ministry, see *Open Doors* by Richard W. Solberg (St. Louis: Concordia, 1992, 240 pages).

2. LWR, through its first 48 years, had just two executive directors. The first was Bernie Confer, who served 36 years, from 1945 until 1981. His successor, Norman Barth, served the next 12. The present executive director, Kathryn Wolford, assumed her present office in the fall of 1993. All three LWR leaders have been lay people. For more on LWR, see Chapter Four and a forthcoming (1995) book by John W. Bachman tracing LWR's half century of work.

3. Much of this section is drawn from "Thirty Years of Anti-Hunger Advocacy" by Patricia L. Kutzner in *Hunger 1994: Transforming the Politics of Hunger* (Silver Spring, Maryland: Bread for the World Institute, 1993).

EMERGENCY APPEALS BECOME PERMANENT

The church body appeals for hunger funds were seen initially as emergency responses to crises in the early 1970s. How did they become permanent fixtures in the overall mission strategies of their churches? The stories are not identical in the three Lutheran bodies (which soon became four, and later two).[1] But there are some common features.

LCMS: Support Across the Spectrum

The Lutheran Church-Missouri Synod was giving renewed attention to hunger exactly when the church was entering a period of major turmoil. The 1969 convention, which had called for sacrificial hunger offerings and established a Commission on World Hunger, had also ousted an incumbent president, replacing him with Dr. J. A. O. Preus. Supporters of the new president made it clear that they expected him to oppose certain theological tendencies in the Synod which they considered unscriptural, particularly among much of the faculty at Concordia Seminary in St. Louis. A four-year struggle surrounding control of that seminary climaxed in early 1974. Its president, John H. Tietjen, was suspended by the seminary board, a majority of the faculty and students continued study "in exile," and a faction of LCMS people called Evangelical Lutherans in Mission began

I believe it's a fact that, during the turbulent 1970s, our World Relief Appeal was the one program which received continuing support from all factions within The Lutheran Church–Missouri Synod.

—Melvin E. Witt

moving toward what would become a separate church less than three years later.

Through all of this, LCMS conventions continued to reaffirm a commitment to combating hunger. Melvin E. Witt, who had become LCMS Secretary of World Relief in 1972, recalls the solid support which the LCMS World Relief/World Hunger Appeal had from all groups within the Synod:

> There was full agreement, across the entire theological spectrum, on the biblical injunction to help hungry people. And the support came from all sides. I believe it's a fact that, during the turbulent 1970s, our World Relief Appeal was the one program which received continuing support from all factions within the LCMS.

Witt notes that his 20 years of experience in the Air Force chaplaincy were valuable preparation for his hunger ministry with the LCMS. (He continued as its World Relief director until 1987, then served two more years full-time and four years part-time as a financial development counselor for LCMS World Relief). "The military chaplaincy taught me to be comfortable in working with other denominations," Witt says, "and much of our hunger activity, both in the U.S. and overseas, was done through ecumenical agencies." Being in the military had also given him an opportunity "to see, up close, the devastating condition of poor and hungry people overseas."

Further, says Witt, his military record was useful "when some of our conservatives thought certain hunger grants—to eastern Europe or to some outspoken Native American groups—were unpatriotic. I could reply with my military credentials, showing I was not anti-U.S."

Witt credits Martin Poch, a former district president who staffed the LCMS World Relief office from 1970 to 1972, with the church's movement into a number of ecumenical hunger organizations. "When I succeeded Martin in 1972, we were helping to support the Commission on Religion in Appalachia, National Indian Lutheran Board, Heifer Project International, and the National Council of Churches' working group on domestic hunger," Witt recalls. "Martin was also a personal friend of Art Simon, the LCMS pastor who was getting Bread for the World launched as a national effort in the mid-seventies, and we supported that movement from the start."

LCMS and Other Lutherans

At its 1975 convention in Anaheim, California, LCMS took several steps toward permanence for its hunger ministry. It terminated the Commission on World Hunger (transferring its duties to the Board of Social Ministry and World Relief), agreed to employ a full-time hunger staff person to assist the World Relief director, and set a goal of a million dollars per year for world hunger, "over and above ongoing World Relief programs."

Subsequent conventions continued to endorse a response to hunger by LCMS people. In 1979, congregations were asked to set a dollar a year per communicant as a goal for world relief/world hunger. The 1981 convention urged members to skip one meal a week and give the cost of it to world relief/world hunger. That convention also encouraged church members to ask their political representatives to place "a higher priority on foreign aid to combat hunger, disease, and poverty" in the developing world. LCMS hunger ministry has been carried out cooperatively with other U.S. Lutherans since the mid-1970s. In May 1975, an LCMS conference in St. Louis included as speakers Francis Moore Lappe', author of *Diet for a Small Planet*, and Dr. James Childs, ethicist at the LCMS senior college in Fort Wayne. Representatives of the ALC and LCA were present as full participants.

A second LCMS hunger seminar in October 1976 included as speakers LWR, ALC, and LCA leaders. Keynoter was Dr. William H. Foege. Raised in an ALC parsonage, then an LCMS medical missionary in Nigeria, in 1977 Foege was named director of the Center for Disease Control in Atlanta. Seminar presentations were gathered into a book, *The Hungry Need Not Die—Unless We Think So*, which was given to all Synod pastors and to LCMS World Relief donors.

"Since all three churches were part of Lutheran World Relief, LWR served as an umbrella for most of our inter-Lutheran work," says Witt. The three churches' hunger staff people, plus the LWR interpretation person, had an initial meeting in April 1975; thereafter, they met regularly to develop common themes and materials. "It made good sense, both eco-nomically and in creativity of ideas," says Witt. "We educated and stimulated each other, and we had no difficulty reaching agreement on the biblical material."

Al Senske, who directed the LCMS World Relief program from 1987 to mid-1994, notes that it "always takes more effort to do anything with other partners. But the pluses of inter-Lutheran cooperation in hunger ministry are obvious. We came up with better ideas, and it's more cost-effective when producing materials and establishing delivery systems." Senske also believes "it's a plus for LCMS members to know that human care minis-try is not the possession of a single church body. When we channel funds through social ministry agencies that are inter-Lutheran, it's good to have other Lutherans also involved."

Its connection with Lutheran World Relief, the joint over-seas agency of LCMS and the ELCA, is helpful in other ways, say LCMS leaders. "The LCMS World Relief program really enjoys a lot of credibility among our members," says Senske. "One reason is that, in the minds of our members, it's tied to Lutheran World Relief, the overseas agency we share with ELCA. Admittedly, some of our people confuse the two because of the similarity in names, but even that confusion often works for good, I believe."

LCMS: U.S. a High Priority

Funds received by LCMS World Relief include those given for domestic and international disaster response. In a year of highly publicized disasters, such as Hurricane Andrew (1992) or the Midwest flooding (1993), total receipts rise significantly.

"Our highest income ever was in the year 1992-93," says Senske, "when both Somalia and Hurricane Andrew were front-page news. Including bequests, we received more than $7,000,000 in that 12-month period." Indications were that giv-ing for the year ending mid-1994, which included response to the massive floods in the Midwest and the southern California earthquake, would exceed $9,000,000—a new record high.

Among the Lutheran bodies, LCMS has normally given the highest percentage of receipts to domestic projects. "After removing the disaster money and administrative costs," Senske explains, "we divide all the rest 40/60: two dollars domestic for every three dollars international."

LCMS annually funds about 100 community development projects in the United States. Included are human care ministries conducted by many kinds of agencies, from congregations (see Chapter One), to Lutheran social ministry organizations, to ecumenical groups. The domestic budget also provides all LCMS support to Lutheran Immigration and Refugee Service (LIRS). Many of the supported ministries are agencies in which the ELCA also participates: national ministries such as LIRS as well as regional Lutheran social ministry organizations and local ecumenical efforts.

"We are seeing LCMS congregations become increasingly involved in addressing human needs on the local level," says Elaine Richter, who succeeded Senske as director of LCMS World Relief in August 1994. "Some of their work is directly congregation-sponsored. Other efforts are through social ministry organizations and inter-Lutheran or interfaith community agencies."

But not all the focus is domestic, of course. Along with its support of LWR and grants to LWF World Service, LCMS World Relief annually channels about $1,000,000 to the Synod's Board for Mission Services for relief and sustainable development through partner churches overseas. LCMS World Relief has also built a strong relationship with the church's women's organization, the Lutheran Women's Missionary League. LCMS women have had a long-standing commitment to making quilts and other parish-project items for LWR overseas distribution. Today, many local women's groups also send direct money gifts to LCMS World Relief.

LCA: Two Years at a Time

The LCA Hunger Appeal was created by its 1974 convention in Baltimore with a two-year life. Initially, it was linked with the LCA Love Compels Action Appeal, a product of that church's response to the urban crises of the 1960s. Robert W. Stackel, hunger appeal director from 1974 to 1980, recalls his frustration with the short time frame:

> Since it was assumed that we were responding to an emergency, which would soon end, the appeal was set up for just

a two-year period. Then it was renewed for another two years in 1976, and for two more in 1978. Finally, in 1980, it was given a 10-year extension.

From the beginning, the dollar response was remarkable. LCA strategy was to set up hunger appeal committees in each of the church's area synods. And the central appeal office was allowed direct access to pastors and congregations; it did not have to go through the LCA's consolidated mailing process. The hunger appeal sent reports on the use of hunger gifts three times yearly to all pastors, and updated synod committees every month.

Of all the Lutheran church bodies, LCA's per-member giving was largest, from the start of its appeal in the mid-seventies. Ed Trexler, editor of LCA's *The Lutheran* magazine, once called the denomination's relationship with its hunger appeal "our church's love affair."

LCA: Binational Program

The LCA hunger funds went to work in several ways. From the beginning, in addition to increasing support for relief and development both at home and abroad, the LCA effort was to include constituency education and "support of governmental programs designed to deal with" the hunger problem.

Funds received were put to work through designated agencies, both LCA and inter-Lutheran. Receipts in the first 15 months (nearly $4,000,000) were used in these proportions: 87% for relief and development overseas, 5% for domestic hunger, and 4% each for education and public-policy advocacy. The LCA would increase the percentages for domestic hunger, education, and advocacy work in future years.

As a binational church, the LCA channeled money for overseas work through both Canadian Lutheran World Relief and the U.S.-based Lutheran World Relief (as well as Lutheran World Federation). The Canadian connection was also used in the 1980s by Vernon Cronmiller. A Canadian, Cronmiller was LCA hunger appeal director from 1980 through 1987. He recalls:

It was clear that U.S. church members weren't as knowledgeable about the world as citizens of a powerful nation need to be. I tried to use my identity as an outsider to say to U.S. people that their nation still needs to learn what being part of the world fully means.

As was true for the LCMS and the ALC, the LCA from the beginning conducted much of its antihunger work with other Lutherans. And once the LCA, the ALC, and the Association of Evangelical Lutheran Churches (AELC) decided in 1982 to plan the creation of a new church, those three bodies worked together more and more in the hunger arena. "We had a good relationship in our hunger work," says Vern Cronmiller. "In many ways we provided a forerunner for the new church. We were able to show people in the pew how a ministry they cared about deeply could be done cooperatively."

ALC: Mostly International

As with the LCA, the ALC's hunger response was initially seen as a short-term enterprise. The 1974 Detroit convention asked ALC members to respond with sacrificial giving for world hunger at Thanksgiving season later that year (a one-time offering) and voted to give to world hunger 50% of an expected surplus in the church's general budget. Further, the ALC asked its president to establish "an ad hoc committee to provide leadership and direction" on world hunger concerns.

The ALC was slow to provide staff resources for its antihunger work. The money response by members and congregations from July through December 1974 was managed by John Brekke, a staff person in the Office of Communication and Mission Support, on a basis of about one-fifth time. The Task Force on World Hunger[2]—as the president's ad hoc committee was named—asked that more staff time be made available and, from the beginning of 1975, Charles P. Lutz of the ALC Division for Life and Mission in the Congregation served half-time as hunger concerns staff.

ALC hunger income in the first two years (summer 1974 through April 1976) totaled $3.75 million. It was used for only two purposes: alleviation of hunger overseas (96%—equal shares through Lutheran World Relief and Lutheran World Federation) and education resources, promotion, and administration (4%).

The 1976 convention (October 6-12, Washington, D.C.) adopted a task force recommendation that, in each of the two years beginning September 1976, the first million dollars be divided: 85% for overseas relief and development, 5% for domestic hunger, and 10% for appeal promotion and constituency education. Funds beyond one million in each year should go entirely overseas.

The task force itself, established for a two-year period, proposed to the 1976 convention that its work be lodged within the regular structures of the ALC and that it be discontinued. A delegate from California, the Rev. George S. Johnson, argued passionately that the task force should continue, but his motion lost. Four years later, Johnson would become staff director of the ALC Hunger Program. The task force was replaced in 1977 by a hunger advisory committee made up of staff and board members from several national units.

The Hunger Program helped to spawn other educational efforts to address poverty and injustice. Perhaps the best-known is the Global Education Center at Augsburg College in Minneapolis, which continues to the present offering experiential learning through overseas study trips.

ALC: Focus on Farmers

Much of the early push for creation of a hunger response within the ALC came from its Committee on Rural Ministries (CORM), a national group which represented agricultural constituencies in the church. CORM had been a central player in the movement which led to 1974 Church Council and General Convention action.

The ALC was known, correctly, as a church with solid rural roots. It was regularly asserted that, among all U.S. church bodies of a million or more members, the ALC had in its membership the highest percentage of family farmers and ranchers. In the 1970s, when the farm population in the nation was barely 3%, it was estimated that persons engaged directly in agriculture comprised as much as 15% of the ALC. It was thus fitting that the ALC's hunger efforts should connect world food concerns with those of its members who were engaged in producing food for the world. This commitment became evident in several ways:

- The 1974 convention action pledged the ALC to "seek new ways of aligning ourselves with farm groups . . ." in addressing the hunger problem.

- Three of the seven-member 1975-76 hunger task force were directly engaged in farming (Robert Bergland, soon to become President Carter's Secretary of Agriculture; Lin Heiller; and Dorothy Hokenstad). And a fourth was a land-grant university agriculture professor (Dale Harpstead).

- The ALC Hunger Program convened consultations of farmers in 1975 (Waverly, Iowa) and 1977 (Kansas City, Missouri). The former issued a much-used statement, "Farmers Speak on World Hunger," and the latter expressed farmers' perspectives on U.S. participation in a proposed international grain reserve.

- The Hunger Program developed "Seven Days of Farming," a popular collection of liturgies linking hunger and the cycles of food production, written by Ewald J. Bash.

- Its hunger coordinator produced a book on ethical issues facing U.S. agriculture, combining hunger concerns and farming practices, which many congregations used as a study document.[3]

The ALC always tried to keep together food for the poor and fairness for U.S. food producers. When the rural economic crisis hit in the 1980s, this linkage would loom especially large.

AELC: A Decade of Devotion

The Association of Evangelical Lutheran Churches (AELC) emerged in late 1976 as a fourth Lutheran body with passion for a ministry to help the hungry. Composed of some 210 former LCMS congregations, it would within six years be planning union with the ALC and the LCA, and within a little more than ten years that new body, the Evangelical Lutheran Church in America, would be constituted. Thus, the AELC did not have a lengthy denominational life, but during its existence of just over a decade, combating hunger was a priority.

"Evangelical Lutherans in Mission, which was a forerunner to the AELC, had launched a hunger appeal already in 1974," says Elwyn Ewald, who served as AELC executive director through its 11 years of life. "We continued that effort. Because we had no hunger staff of our own, we basically used materials produced by the ALC and LCA. While the money from our 100,000 members was not large—averaging only about $100,000 a year—I was pleased that about 80% of our congregations annually participated in the appeal."

More than 90% of the AELC hunger dollars went to work overseas, Ewald recalls. Equal portions were channeled through Lutheran World Relief and Lutheran World Federation. At home, the AELC was a solid promoter of Bread for the World, consistently making an annual grant to that organization.

As a member of the commission which planned the ELCA, 1982-87, and with a strong personal interest in hunger, Ewald played an influential role in shaping ELCA mechanisms for hunger ministry. "We tried to plot a middle course," he says, "between the LCA's pattern of distributing responsibility among several churchwide offices and the ALC's approach, which was more focused in the church-in-society unit. We said hunger functions and funds should be handled by several ELCA divisions, but that Church in Society should have a strong coordinating role."

That pattern has continued through the ELCA's first seven years. And, in the judgment of nearly all observers, antihunger activity is a clear success story for the new church.

For Discussion

1. Read Luke 4:18-19. What is it saying to the people of God in your congregation today?

2. Concerning Dr. Witt's comment at the head of this chapter: Why is it that hunger ministries are able to unite Christians of widely differing theological viewpoints? What does it mean to the group that Lutherans from church bodies not in doctrinal agreement seem to work well together in responding to hunger?

3. Discuss Vern Cronmiller's comment about U.S. citizens' knowledge of world affairs. Do you agree that citizens of smaller nations (such as Canada) often have a more highly developed awareness of global realities? What are some reasons that U.S. citizens may have less interest in international issues?

4. What special credibility do you think farmers and ranchers have on hunger issues? If they are not present in your membership, what are some ways your congregation might build a relationship with food producers? Consider this question again, replacing "farmers and ranchers" with "those who are or have been hungry."

END NOTES

1. Some 210 former LCMS congregations organized the Association of Evangelical Lutheran Churches (AELC) as a new church body in December 1976. The Evangelical Lutheran Church in America was constituted by the AELC, ALC, and LCA in May 1987; it began functioning as a new body on January 1, 1988.

2. President David W. Preus appointed to the ALC's hunger task force, in late 1974, *Bruce Howe*, attorney in Dickinson, North Dakota, chair; *L. David Brown*, pastor in Waverly, Iowa; *Dale D. Harpstead*, professor and chair of soil sciences, Michigan State University, East Lansing, Michigan; *Lin Heiller,* beef and grain producer in Melvin, Iowa; *Dorothy Hokenstad*, farm homemaker in Garretson, South Dakota; *Martin O. Sabo*, speaker of the Minnesota House of Representatives, St. Paul; and *Fredrik A. Schiotz*, president emeritus of the ALC, Minneapolis. *Congressman Robert Bergland* of Minnesota's 7th District, Roseau, replaced Sabo in early 1975.

3. *Farming the Lord's Land*, edited by Charles P. Lutz with foreword by Robert Bergland (Minneapolis: Augsburg, 1980).

IT'S ABOUT
PEOPLE FISHING

There's a saying in many cultures around the world: "Give people fish and you feed them for today; teach people to fish and they will be fed for many tomorrows." The church's response to a hungry world has always sought to do both. There is direct feeding of people who, without that food, would starve—if not today then very shortly after today. But there is also a commitment to end the direct aid as soon as possible and move into another mode: helping people to become more self-reliant.

How do you teach people to fish when their shoreline is a conflict zone? How do you teach people to fish when their waters are polluted from the textile factories [upstream]? How do you teach people to plow where they do not own the land? How do you teach people to plant when the only seeds they have available are those from the North requiring insecticides and fertilizers they cannot afford?

—Lani Havens

The old folk saying lifts up the tension between emergency response and support for longer-range solutions. Our shorthand terms for these two kinds of activity are *relief* and *development*. Both words have found their way into the names of church and other agencies which are addressing hunger and poverty. We have Lutheran World *Relief* and LCMS World *Relief* and Catholic *Relief* Services. We have the Overseas *Development* Council and the Ecumenical *Development* Cooperative Society. U.S. Roman Catholics have their

Campaign for Human *Development,* and the former American
Lutheran Church had its *Development* Assistance Program.

Relief, Development, and More

The fact is, a well-rounded response to hunger requires both
relief and development. And it requires even more. A complete
response demands attention to the factors that keep poor people
from fishing at all, as the quotation by Lani Havens at the head
of this chapter suggests. Havens, who was executive director of
Church World Service from 1990 to 1993, is pointing to the
need for fundamental changes in political and economic systems
that lock people into poverty. Alleviating hunger, she is saying,
will first require significantly reducing war or environmental
degradation or landlessness or unfairness in global trade.

That third mode of hunger response has been called systemic change, or transformation, or liberation, or even simple
justice. For most of us in the churches, it has been more difficult
than relief and development . . . more difficult to understand,
certainly. But also more difficult to accept because, if we are
among the comfortable minority of the world's people, we think
systemic change might make us losers. Finally, it's more difficult
to know which system-change efforts will make any difference.
How can we, as U.S. church members or as citizens, exert any
meaningful impact on land-tenure policies in El Salvador, or on
the world market price received by a Tanzanian coffee farmer?
For that matter, most of us feel quite powerless about what to do
concerning the underlying causes of poverty in our own land.

We'll return, later in this chapter, to the system-change
question. Meanwhile, the reality is that most of the churches'
resources for combating hunger continue to go for either relief
or development. How are we trying to address both? How are
they interconnected, yet separate? And what are the
current trends?

A Remarkable Shift

Many observers think the biggest change among U.S. church
people in our understanding of hunger over the past quarter
century has been our movement from a relief mentality to a
development mentality. "My chief impression of that period,"

says Pastor Vernon Cronmiller, who worked with the hunger appeals of both the Lutheran Church in America and the Evangelical Lutheran Church in America, "is the change in understanding among the people of God. Instead of thinking emergency response, we now see ourselves as working much more with the development of peoples."

Elaine Richter says the same of changes in the work of LCMS World Relief. "We're doing more in development, along with relief," she reports. "Both our overseas efforts and disaster response in the U.S. regularly evolve into continuing, sustainable development activities."

Kathryn Wolford, executive director of Lutheran World Relief, says that "more than half of the church dollars flowing through LWR go to development." In a typical year, LWR receives about $6,000,000 from its two member church bodies, plus another $2,000,000 or more in direct gifts, mostly from Lutheran individuals. In addition to money, LWR receives from church members large quantities of material aid—quilts, clothing, kits for infants and schoolchildren—which are distributed overseas in both emergency and long-term projects.[1]

Relief typically means getting immediate food or shelter or clothing or medical help to people who have been struck by a calamity. The disaster may be natural (as with a drought or earthquake) or it may be human-caused (such as war or environmental degradation). Development typically involves such activities as food production or environmental restoration or literacy training or job generation or health education or empowerment of women or community organizing—and often all of that and more in the same project.

If the churches' goal really is to alleviate *hunger*, giving more resources to development than to relief is surely the wise approach. It is estimated that, in any given year, only about 10% to 15% of hunger in the world results from emergencies; most hunger, 85% to 90%, is born from chronic poverty.[2]

Relief and Development: the Interplay

Relief and development should not be seen as competing modes of response to poor and hungry people. Rather, they are complementary. Certainly there are occasions when an emergency requires a relief response and there is no follow-up development work. Getting aid to the Kurds in northern Iraq and southeastern Turkey after the Persian Gulf War would be a recent example. The world's Lutherans were heavily involved in immediate aid to the Kurds for a few months in 1991; when that effort ended, Lutherans did not take part in subsequent development activity. Another example from the 1990s, relief to Bosnian Muslims in the former Yugoslavia, may or may not be succeeded by development work.

Says Kathryn Wolford, LWR executive director, regarding activity that is directly related to hostilities:

> Increasingly, our work either results from or is complicated by religious and ethnic conflicts. Our goal is to respond to human suffering wherever it occurs, without taking or even appearing to take sides. The deeper challenge in such complex situations is to ensure that humanitarian aid is not inadvertently enabling the warring parties to prolong the conflict. Good intentions must be accompanied by thoughtful analysis.

But whatever the cause of a particular calamity—whether human activity or natural disaster—relief and development seem often to come as the twin offspring of a given tragedy that befalls people.

One common scenario is *development following relief.* In 1971, civil war erupted between the eastern and western portions of Pakistan. The fighting was in the east and many residents fled across the border into India, where Lutheran World Federation provided emergency assistance. When hostilities ended, the independent nation of Bangladesh was established and refugees returned home. In the northwest corner of the country, home of many who had been refugees, community leaders asked LWF World Service to stay on with the people, helping them to resettle and rebuild their lives. LWF agreed. What had been a relief effort—Rangpur Dinajpur Refugee Service—became Rangpur Dinajpur Rural Service, a comprehensive development program which continues to the present day. Major amounts of U.S. world hunger/world relief funds have gone to work there in the past two decades.

Another pattern is *development alongside relief*. When starvation faced Somalians in 1992-93, LWF again was a major actor among the world's responding voluntary agencies, airlifting food from Kenya for many months. LWF received support for that relief activity from U.S. Lutherans, including grants from Lutheran World Relief. But the latter agency also saw an opportunity to address longer-term needs. LWR invested several hundred thousand dollars in water development projects in Somalia's northeast. It is a dramatic example of development happening parallel to a massive relief effort.

Finally, there is *development without relief*. One can find numerous instances of development efforts among peoples and communities whose crisis is the ongoing one of chronic poverty, but with no dramatic emergency calling for a relief response. In four communities of indigenous Guatemalans, for example, LWR is investing about $27,000 annually in 1994 and 1995. The money will help 630 people to create improved health services and income-generating activities.

Where in the World Are We?

"We've come to see that handouts are not the way to help people," says Dr. Robert Marshall, a former president of the LCA who left the LWR board of directors in 1994 after 25 years, the last 16 of them as its president. "We simply must help people to help themselves, and there's a growing awareness that people must be involved from the start in defining their problems and what will work to change things."

It has long been part of the churches' development theory that local people must have a major voice in shaping development efforts in their communities. And the definition of development continues to be refined. In the early 1980s, for example, LWR began asking of every project it considered, "Does it take seriously the role of women?" Since the early nineties, LWR has insisted that sustainability be a central component of its projects.

At any given time, U.S. Lutheran world relief/world hunger gifts are working to undergird the development of peoples in about 50 of the world's countries. Nearly all of the locations are in Asia, Africa, Latin America, and the Middle

East. Exceptions would be the occasional natural disaster else-where in the world (e.g., an earthquake in Armenia/Azerbaijan) or a war zone such as the former Yugoslavia.

LWR in a typical year supports between 150 and 200 pro-jects in about 40 countries. LWF World Service in 1993 had long-term development under way in 20 countries and emer-gency activity in another seven. In many cases, LWR and LWF can be counted in the same countries, the U.S. agency giving financial support to work that is carried out by LWF.[3]

There is gradual shifting in the locales. Major money went to development in South Korea and Taiwan, for example, in the 1950s and sixties—none goes there today, since those are no longer areas of great need. And within large nations there can be movement from less to more impoverished areas; in India, for example, LWR decided in the early 1990s to concentrate on the six poorest states. There is but one area of the world—Pales-tine—in which LWR and LWF World Service have been involved continually from the onset of hostilities almost half a century ago.

To complete the picture, world relief/world hunger money is also working overseas through the global mission units of the U.S. Lutheran bodies. Both LCMS and ELCA consistently chan-nel portions of their international development funds through partner churches or missionary personnel overseas. A substantial share of the support of agricultural development specialists, for example, is provided by world hunger/world relief funds.

Here at Home?

In work with domestic hunger, the great majority of the resources provided by the national churches has gone for devel-opment. "Our grants for domestic hunger are divided approximately 80% development, 20% relief," says John Halvor-son, coordinator of the ELCA Hunger Program.

It was similar in the ELCA predecessor bodies. The ALC made grants for domestic hunger through a churchwide approach called "Development Assistance Program" (DAP). Almost none of those grants supported feeding programs or direct material assistance to poor people. "We encouraged our church people to support such efforts right in their own com-munities," says George Johnson, ALC Hunger Program director from 1980 to 1987. "There was no point in congregations sending money for local food shelves to the national office and then our having to send it back."

DAP, established during the urban crises of the late sixties, from 1975 onward had both regular benevolence money and hunger dollars to distribute, averaging about $500,000 a year from the two sources. It concentrated on seed-money grants (up to two years), in the range of $2,500 to $7,500, for projects that were development or system-change oriented.

Domestic-hunger funding by the LCA was similar. "Most of our grants were for development," says Arnold Tiemeyer, who directed that activity for the LCA Division for Mission in North America. "They were typically in the range of $5,000 to $25,000. We responded, based on our criteria, to requests that came in. We tried to respond especially to tough urban settings in the Northeast and to rural communities." Tiemeyer notes that the LCA sought to tie local LCA members into an enduring relationship with a project whenever possible.

Tiemeyer recalls that the quality and persistence of on-site leadership was usually the key factor in a project's success. "Where local leadership stays for the long haul, a solid product can result. I think of Mary Nelson in Chicago [see Chapter Six] or John Steinbruck in D.C. [see Chapter One]. More often, I'm afraid, the leaders graduate out of a poor urban community. When that happens, the leaders may have won, but the community loses."

Both LCA and ALC also invested major hunger funds in broad community-economic-development activities. One was the Nehemiah Project in New York City, a church-sponsored effort to provide housing for low-income people; both LCMS and ELCA continue to be involved with Nehemiah. Another was a MESBIC (Minority Enterprise Small Business Investment Corporation) through the Alabama Rural Council, which was intended to generate jobs for poor people. The Nehemiah Project has had significant success; the Alabama venture failed, largely because the promise of federal government matching funds was never fulfilled.

And Beyond Development?

What about that third mode: seeing that people can fish without being shot at, can have access to fishing waters that are unpolluted, and can find a fair price for their surplus catch?[4]

Says Robert Marshall: "Lutheran World Relief has learned that, in a conflict situation, development efforts alone are self-defeating. Attention must be given to peace and reconciliation." During his years as executive director of LWR (1981-93), Norman Barth strongly supported the agency's involvement in the quest for resolution of armed conflicts. "One thing LWR can do is press the U.S. government toward tension-reducing measures," he says. "In the Middle East, for example, we need to insist on economic assistance and policies that will reduce the militarization of the region."

LWR in recent years has itself given modest support to peacemaking efforts, usually in settings where it has already been doing development work. It co-sponsored an all-Africa conference on "The Role of Religious Leaders in Peacemaking and Social Change." It has enabled Sudanese church representatives to take part in consultations regarding peace in the Sudan. In Beit Sahour, near Bethlehem, a small LWR grant helped the Rapprochement Center to enhance understandings among Muslims, Jews, and Christians. In Nicaragua, LWR has supported the efforts of the Evangelical Committee for Development (CEPAD), its partner agency, to train community-level peace and reconciliation commissions. LWR also provided support to churches and grassroots groups in Guatemala for developing joint proposals for achieving peace, justice, and development in that war-ravaged nation.

LWF, too, has assisted the peacemaking process, perhaps most notably in Guatemala during recent years. Over its five decades of existence, LWF has been active in pressing for political solutions in many of the planet's war zones, including Namibia and South Africa, the Middle East, and the former Yugoslavia.

Development That Is Sustainable

It has become increasingly clear that food security for people is closely linked to protecting the earth's ability to provide our food. Indeed, a growing body of global analysts believes that wars and civil violence in the future will result chiefly from environmental factors: battles over water, cropland, forests, fish. Environmental stress and high population growth will combine to cause both hunger and group-against-group violence.[5] And it seems undeniable that many of us today are able to feed ourselves only because we are borrowing against our children's sources of food.

World relief/world hunger resources obviously have a growing role to play in caring for creation. As Dr. Job Ebenezer, director of environmental stewardship and hunger education for the ELCA, puts it:

> The true measure of development must be other than growth in gross national product per-capita. Often when a country's GNP rises, environmental protection declines, and so does the quality of life for many citizens. Development modeled on the Western pattern tends to ignore its cost to the environment. Development that is sustainable, however, always counts care of the earth as a central factor.

"Sustainable development" can be defined as "using the earth's resources so as to provide an acceptable quality of life for present generations without compromising the quality of life for future generations." LWR now requires that environmental sustainability be at the heart of all the projects it supports. The goal is to identify with efforts that combine three elements: addressing basic needs of the poorest people, doing so by empowering grassroots communities, and always protecting their environment for future generations.

That means in Peru, for example, that LWR is working with local groups to support agro-ecology, a holistic approach to agriculture which uses environment-friendly methods. The approach includes a return to the methods employed by indigenous people, before the Europeans arrived five centuries ago. It means supporting in Kenya small-scale organic farmers and the spread of hand-operated seed-oil presses and the promotion of solar cookers.

And in the Philippines' southern island of Mindanao, LWR is providing $265,000 for a three-year project that is helping 240 highland farm families. Each family is acquiring a five-acre plot of government-owned land under a 25-year "stewardship agreement." The project involves farmers in water and soil conservation activities and in seeking a ban on area logging, which has produced rapid forest depletion and erosion via illegal operations. With technical and financial resources from both governmental and nongovernmental agencies, farmers are expected to increase food production by 10% over the three-year period. Arranged through the Philippines Department of Energy and Natural Resources, the project is managed by a national companion agency of LWR, the Philippine Partnership for Development of Human Resources in Rural Areas.

Environment-friendly Behavior

"We are also looking for innovative ways of helping our church members here at home to adopt behavior that is more environment-friendly," says Ebenezer, whose environmental-stewardship program is supported largely by world hunger funds. "A small grant to a community-supported agriculture project in Minnesota (named Common Harvest) gives Lutherans a chance to participate in food production that has earth-stewardship at its core. It is also a way of discouraging reliance on importing food from low-income countries, or transporting vegetables thousands of miles in our own country."

The ELCA environmental stewardship program also encourages congregations to develop their own gardens: to provide items for local food pantries and even to raise the flowers and plants they use in liturgical settings and for members' birthdays and other anniversaries. And this program helps parishes to reduce their energy consumption. "The average congregation can save at least $100 a month, through simple changes in lighting and heating," says Ebenezer. "The result will be to reduce the church's contribution to the emission of carbon dioxide while also freeing dollars for ministries that are more vital than support of the local utility company."

Learning about environmental responsibility is not a new emphasis in the churches, of course. Leaders of outdoor ministries, for example, were among the first to connect food and care of creation, from the mid-1970s onward. Pastor Duane Hanson, director of Bethel Horizons Camp of Bethel Lutheran Church in Madison, Wisconsin, recalls:

> Our camp had farmland and in about 1975 we developed a
> Food Village. We saw to it that both campers and staff had

their hands in the soil for several hours each week. We related gardening to Bible stories on hunger and stewardship of creation. We brought in guests, including furloughing missionaries, who would tie our emphasis to their overseas locales. That program continued for about 10 years, and then we moved naturally into environmental education, which continues to this day.

Approaches to hunger based on behavior changes among the nonhungry come, of course, in many varieties. And most of them require involvement in political processes. How hunger ministries have become part of politics is a large subject, large enough to have its own chapter in this book. The politics of helping people to gain access to fishing, to keep their waters unpolluted, and to be free to market their surplus catch—all of this appears as Chapter Five.

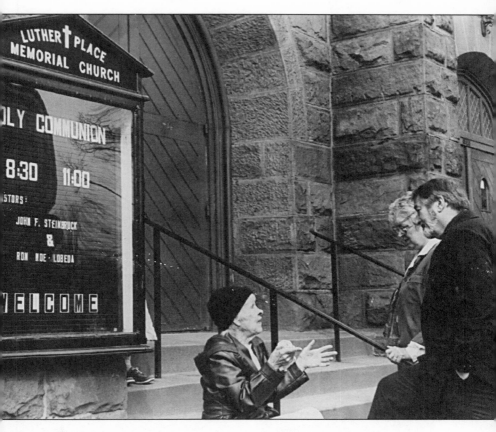

A. *PASTOR JOHN STEINBRUCK and Erna Steinbruck (center) of Luther Place Church (ELCA) in Washington, D.C., visit with a street person at church entrance (Paula Wolfson photo).*

CREATIVE CONGREGATIONS

B. *PASTOR JULIO A. LOZA at Comedor Popular Soup Kitchen, St. Matthew Lutheran Church (LCMS), Chicago.*

C. *THE MUELLERS, Howard and Fran (center) of St. Paul Lutheran Church (ELCA) in Waverly, Iowa, visit with a friend.*

D. *SERVANT EVENT youth group, with LCMS World Relief support, installs septic system for disabled Appalachian family.*

E. *BRYAN HUNTZIN-GER of Grace Lutheran Church (ELCA) in Des Moines, Washington, led Grace high schoolers in work at Hispanic ministry building project (1993 photo by Jeffrey High).*

F. *IN KERALA STATE, southwest India, village community health workers during a break in their training program. Lutheran World Relief assisted this project in late 1980s (1988 photo by Charles P. Lutz).*

G. *IN GHANA, west Africa, reforestation funded by LCMS World Relief is integral part of LCMS mission work at Nasuan Development Centre.*

PROJECTS AND PEOPLE

H. *IN NORTHWEST BANGLADESH, human power oper-
ates treadle pump to bring water to rice fields; technology was
introduced by Rangpur Dinajur Rural Service, development
project supported by global Lutheran community through LWF
(1988 photo by Charles P. Lutz).*

I. *IN EAST JERUSALEM, Augusta Victoria Hospital has been
operated by Lutheran World Federation since late 1940s, serving
primarily Palestinian people (1991 photo by Charles P. Lutz).*

J. *IN PERU, Lutheran World Relief supports reintroduction and improvement of alpacas and llamas; the animals provide wool and meat, also serve as beasts of burden. Here, Peruvian woman spins wool from family's alpacas (Kathryn Wolford photo).*

K. *IN GUATEMALA, political violence has left many widows. Via an organic gardening project in the Ixil Triangle, Lutheran World Relief helps some of them to improve nutrition and to heal the earth (Kathryn Wolford photo).*

L. *IN SALINA, Kansas, quilts, school kits, and other materials produced through parish projects are loaded for shipment to Lutheran World Relief warehouse in Minneapolis.*

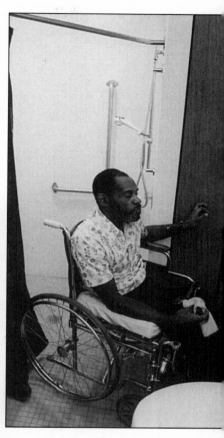

M. *IN CLEVELAND, living facilities for persons with disabilities are remodeled through Metropolitan Lutheran Ministries, assisted by LCMS World Relief.*

N. *IN CHICAGO, Walther Leaguers at St. Luke's Lutheran Church (LCMS) sorted clothing for LWR to send to Middle East following 1967 Six-Day War.*

O. IN TANZANIA, husband and wife were able to buy a sunflower oilseed press through project funded by Lutheran World Relief. Seeds are drying in sun, which increases yield of oil (Dallas Granima photo).

P. BISHOP L. DAVID BROWN (right) of Iowa visits with Bishop Kleopas Dumeni of Namibia, in northern Namibia (1986 photo by Charles P. Lutz).

Q. IN MAHARASHTRA STATE, westcentral India, the Arole doctors— Maybelle (left) and Raj—at their Comprehensive Rural Health Project in Jamkhed. Lutheran World Relief for many years provided financial support for the work of these Lutheran physicians (1988 photo by Charles P. Lutz).

R. *IN NIGER'S Tagazar Valley, wire fencing is made to provide work and income through Welldiggers Association of Niger, supported by Lutheran World Relief (1994 photo by Charles P. Lutz).*

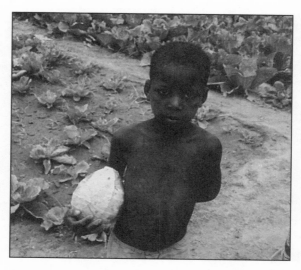

S. *IN NIGER, west Africa, cabbage is produced by community garden, supported through Lutheran World Relief (1994 photo by Charles P. Lutz).*

T. *IN IVORY COAST, west Africa, sewing class for Liberian refugees, organized by LCMS missionary and funded by LCMS World Relief.*

U. *KATHRYN WOLFORD, executive director of Lutheran World Relief since 1993, with her predecessor in that position, Norman Barth (1993 photo by Charles P. Lutz).*

V. *ARTHUR SIMON, founding president of Bread for the World, 1974-91.*

W. *DAVID BECKMANN, president of Bread for the World since 1991.*

MAKING A DIFFERENCE

X. DOROTHY BORGE
of Conrad, Montana.

Y. *AL RODRIGUEZ (left) and Virgil Armendariz Jr. display Nebraska
driver manuals, which they lobbied to have produced in non-English lan-
guages* (**Omaha World Herald** *photo by Fred Veleba*).

Z. DONALD NELSEN *(right)*
of Copeland, Kansas, sacking
potatoes to help feed low-income
families.

AA. NORMA MARKS *(left) and Mildred Grady of Pompano Beach,*
Florida.

BB. *KEN PETERSON of Tamarack, Minnesota, with friend at Faith and Hope Refugee Camp, El Salvador, in 1984.*

CC. *MARY NELSON of Bethel New Life, west Chicago (left).*

DD. *JEANNE COR-DOVA of Roadrunner for Christ, Denver.*

For Discussion

1. Read Psalm 104. Note who, according to the psalmist, is creation's basic provider. What does the psalm suggest are the features of God's design for a world in which the needs of all living things are met?

2. While development receives by far the larger part of the church's human-care resources, relief seems to get much more media attention. Why is that so? Does it matter?

3. Maimonides, the 12th-century Jewish philosopher, is credited with formulating "The Eight Degrees of Charity":

   a) Giving to the poor, but with bad grace.

   b) Giving with good grace, but not enough.

   c) Giving enough, but only after being asked.

   d) Giving enough, but without being asked.

   e) Giving without knowing who will benefit from the gift.

   f) Giving without the beneficiary knowing who is the giver.

   g) Giving without knowing who will benefit and without the beneficiary knowing who is the giver.

   h) Giving so the poor have the means by which they may permanently escape from poverty.

Talk about Maimonides' progression in relation to relief, development, and systemic change. Tie your discussion to the ideas presented in the grid of Appendix C.

4. Discuss ways in which alleviating hunger and caring for the creation must go together. Give some specific examples—from your own region and around the planet. What changes do you think are needed in the ways human beings use the earth?

END NOTES

1. Since about 1990, the basic church support of LWR and LWF World Service has come entirely from world hunger/world relief funds, whereas previously the churches provided core support to those agencies from their general benevolence budgets. "It is to be regretted that the churches have been unable to continue supporting the core administrative costs of LWR from regular benevolence funds," says Robert Marshall. At times of major emergencies, LWR also becomes a channel for substantial U.S. government aid overseas, and probably 90% of that resource goes for direct relief purposes.

2. See "A Post-Rio Compact" by James Gustave Speth, president of World Resources Institute, in the Fall 1992 issue of *Foreign Policy*.

3. For treatment of the distinction between LWR and LWF, see Chapter Two.

4. In 1975, the author developed a teaching tool on the modes of relief, development, and systemic change. It appears as Appendix C.

5. See Robert D. Kaplan's article, "The Coming Anarchy," in the February 1994 *Atlantic Monthly.*

CHANGING THE NONHUNGRY

Alleviating hunger in our world means, in extreme situations, that those who are hungry must be given food immediately. In other situations, it means assisting the hungry to have the means for producing or acquiring their own food. We typically identify these modes as *relief* and *development*.

Both focus on doing things for and with hungry people. Those of us who are not hungry can do both "out of our abundance" and "in our spare time," so to speak. To most of us, the cost in either dollars or hours is slight. (For some marvelous exceptions to that generalization, see Chapter Six.) What church people do collectively to combat hunger through relief and development activities is indeed substantial—our numbers make it quantitatively impressive. But few of us would claim that our support for relief and development efforts is responding "sacrificially" (as the 1969 LCMS convention asked); few would argue that we are making the "sacrifices [that] will be required" (President Gerald Ford's speech to 1974 ALC convention, see Chapter Two).

> *In advocacy for hungry people, it is the churches that have become the long-distance runners.*
>
> —Larry Minear

Beyond Relief and Development

From the beginning, the churches' hunger ministries have recognized that lifting people out of hunger will require more than changing the immediate reality of hungry people. To return to the fishing imagery: learning how to fish won't end my hunger

if I'm denied access to the water, or discover the water is polluted, or have no market for my surplus catch, or find my
fishing spots are in the middle of a war zone.

Thus, for many of the hungry to have food, changes need
to happen among those who are *not* hungry: changes that go
beyond increasing our charity, changes in how the comfortable
ones of this planet think and act as economic and political
beings. In other words, changes in the systems will be needed, so
those systems benefit the many as well as the few.

The initial hunger-ministry goals of the LCMS and the
ELCA (as well as its predecessor bodies) included education and
political advocacy. In its 1969 convention action, LCMS urged
members to contact federal government representatives about
hunger and the need "to reassess national values and priorities."
The 1974 LCA convention called for "sensitizing the church's
constituency to the nature and extent of the crisis" and "critical
address to governmental programs" dealing with hunger.

Educational Resources

A small percentage of hunger giving has consistently been used
by the churches for educational tools. As early as 1976, the
LCMS, LCA, and ALC—through their Coordinating Committee
for Cooperative Parish Education Projects—produced a five-ses-
sion adult study, "Hope for Hungry Human Beings." Many
other educational resources for all ages—print, film, video,
games—soon followed. Lutherans also took part in regional
hunger conferences which were planned ecumenically in many
areas of the nation.

"On development education," says George Johnson, ALC
hunger program director in the 1980s, "I feel we could have
done better. Some progress in global education has been made
in our church colleges and seminaries. But I wish we had made
better use of people at state universities who were specialists in
global concerns. And we could have done more to share the
excellent materials provided by Lutheran World Federation and
the World Council of Churches." Johnson believes the LWF
Office of Research and Social Action (now Research and Development Education), directed by a South African, Sibusiso
Bengu, was especially creative in helping the northern-world

churches to hear the voices of developing-world Christians. (Bengu became minister of education in the inter-racial cabinet named by South African President Nelson Mandela in 1994.)

Another aspect of development education for Lutherans, Johnson notes, has been "examining the emphases of Lutheran theology itself. As traditionally presented, it did not give people much permission to address justice issues." Johnson believes that, in recent years, U.S. Lutherans have become more willing "to see working for justice as our direct response to God's work in our justification."

How We Consume

Changing the consumption patterns of the well-fed and economically comfortable has been a central emphasis in the churches' hunger education over the past two decades. A biblical theology of enough was articulated, and themes such as these became common: Eat lower on the food chain (more grains, less meat); skip one meal a week and give the money saved to combat hunger; reduce your energy consumption, especially in fossil-fuels.

In the lifestyle simplification movement, two books by British authors were especially influential: E. F. Schumacher's *Small Is Beautiful* and John V. Taylor's *Enough Is Enough* (whose North American edition was published by Augsburg, with the encouragement of the ALC Hunger Program, in 1977).

Alternatives, a church-sponsored agency working on questions of lifestyle simplification, was supported by Lutheran hunger funds from its beginnings in the 1970s. It is perhaps best known for its focus on less-consumerist ways of celebrating Christmas and other holidays.

From a Manhattan Parish

But changes in the thinking and the consuming of nonhungry people are not the end of it. The central goal of those who seek change by and among the economically comfortable is a conversion in our political behavior. It is surprising that Lutherans, not known generally for political activism, have been among the leaders in the hunger-and-politics arena. Indeed, George Johnson believes "it was hunger that helped many of our church members to get politically active for the first time, and from it they entered other social concerns as well."

This hunger/politics arena has two rings; they share an
agenda and many of the actors are the same, but the rings are
also distinct. One is the circle of formal involvement in public-
policy work by *the church as institution*. The other is the circle
where church members *as individual citizens* seek to influence
public policy.

In the latter circle, the most important development of the
past quarter century, without question, has been the creation of
Bread for the World (BFW). The idea for what became BFW
took shape in the mind of the pastor of Trinity Lutheran
Church, a small LCMS congregation on Manhattan's Lower East
Side. That pastor was Arthur Simon and his idea evolved in the
midst of Trinity's ministry among people who were economically
poor.

Simon, who had been serving at Trinity since 1961, recalls
that Trinity held a series of hunger discussions following mid-
week worship in Lent of 1969. Trinity congregation then
prepared a hunger resolution for consideration at the LCMS
national convention to be held that July. The Synod's response
to that resolution and other, similar overtures was to create a
Commission on World Hunger (see Chapter Two). A few years
later, Art Simon co-authored a book, *The Politics of World Hunger*,
with his brother Paul, then lieutenant governor of Illinois and
now a U.S. senator from that state. Art remembers:

> After the manuscript was at the publisher, it occurred to me
> that political action by church members was the missing piece
> in the churches' response to hunger. Could we create some-
> thing like Common Cause with a faith base? I tried out the
> idea with some people I respected, including Gerhard Elston,
> a Lutheran working in international affairs for the National
> Council of Churches, and Pastor Richard John Neuhaus, at
> St. John the Evangelist Lutheran Church (LCMS) in Brook-
> lyn. William J. Byron, a Jesuit with the Woodstock Com-
> munity, was another. All were supportive. We organized first
> in the New York area, in March 1973, and we used the name
> "Bread for the World."

BFW began organizing nationwide one year later. "Our
goal from the outset was to try to get at the underlying causes of

hunger and poverty through better national policies," says
Simon, "and to do that intentionally as a response to the gospel.
The churches were doing an outstanding job of assisting people
through their relief and development agencies, but almost nothing was being done to invite Christians to be responsible *as
citizens* in addressing hunger." Yet, Simon notes, "One stroke of
the President's pen or one vote in Congress often has an impact
on hungry people that far exceeds anything we do through all
of U.S. private assistance."

An early question facing Bread for the World's founders
was whether its basis should be interfaith, or no faith, or Christian faith. "We decided our task was to reach people in the
churches," Simon notes, "and explicit biblical content has been
central to our approach. Worship and Bible study have helped
to nurture the movement from the start, though our approach
to government leaders is always couched in secular policy
language."

ALC and BFW

After a few years of organizing in Congressional districts nationwide, BFW's membership plateaued in the 45,000 range, not
large for a lobbying organization. But its influence and respect—
with the federal government, in the nongovernmental advocacy
community, and in the churches—is large indeed. Its legislative
successes, achieved in coalition with other advocacy groups, have
been many. They range from passage of its initial Right-to-Food
Resolution in 1976 to the Africa Relief and Recovery Act in
1984 to expansion of funding for domestic food programs in
the 1990s.

Many church members and others who have not formally
joined BFW do become involved in its work. Its annual offering
of letters, for example, generates communications to members
of Congress which number in the hundreds of thousands.
Always focused on a single legislative proposal, the letters, in
some congregations, are gathered at offering time and presented, along with that week's money gifts, as a response to God.
Next day, they are mailed to the respective U.S. representatives
and senators. In other congregations, members receive background information and respond individually.

"The idea came from a participant in that 1969 Lenten discussion at Trinity Church," says Simon. "Her name was Gik Schmidt."

Lutherans have been disproportionately supportive of BFW from its earliest days. "All the Lutheran church bodies made annual grants from the very first," says Simon. "Martin Poch of the LCMS Board for World Relief was a strong supporter. But the most powerful early boost was an endorsement letter which Presiding Bishop David Preus sent to all ALC pastors. It brought a great response: the ALC for years thereafter had twice as many Bread members as all other Lutherans combined."[1] In 1994, BFW reported that Lutheran congregations accounted for fully one-third of its 1,000 covenant churches.

When Art Simon left BFW's presidency in the fall of 1991, the organization asked another LCMS-trained pastor to replace him. David Beckmann, schooled in economics as well as theology, had previously served at the World Bank for 15 years; his last position there was senior advisor on nongovernmental organizations. In 1975-76, Beckmann had worked for LWF World Service in Bangladesh. He is now on the ELCA clergy roster.

Post-Cold War: Who Cares?
Beckmann says the political will to deal with world hunger is weak in this post-Cold War period. "Now that there's no need to keep the Russians out, we feel no need to woo the less-developed countries any more," he observes. "Supporting foreign aid for the truly poor is counter to the current cultural and political climate in this country. The churches aren't doing enough, but compared to other institutions they're doing quite a bit. And Bread for the World continues to be one of the major advocates of aid to the genuinely needy."

As the world's sole remaining superpower, the United States has both the ability and the responsibility to take the lead in addressing the global rich-poor gap, Beckmann believes. "Yet, the developing countries are on the Clinton Administration's back burner," Beckmann says. Unhappy about the leadership provided by Presidents of both parties on world hunger, he says it's up to U.S. church members to make a difference:

> Rarely does a President take a position regarding the developing countries, in a campaign or a State of the Union

message, which is other than self-interested. And church members simply aren't insisting on any other stance. In my view, world poverty and hunger will not be reduced unless U.S. Christians become far more assertive in communicating concern for the earth's hungry people. We need to see our political witness as a key part of our evangelical witness.

Overall, Beckmann believes Lutherans have a relatively good record on hunger, for a couple of reasons. "We have lots of people with roots in farm country," he notes, "and that has given our church a gut feeling for land and food concerns. Further, the gospel really does make a difference among us. We understand God's grace and want to show our gratitude by helping others."

BFW is "woven into the fabric of the ELCA more than is true with any other denomination," Beckmann says. "The Presbyterians would be a close second." Beckmann thinks Lutherans like BFW because "it stays close to Bible language. It's one of the few Christian movements which is able to bring a very wide range of Christians—from Pentecostals to high-church Episcopalians—under the same tent."

LCA and the States

If the ALC led in Lutheran support of Bread for the World, the LCA was clearly the leader in another advocacy arena. Addressing governmental programs was an LCA hunger objective from the start. The LCA devoted a substantial portion of appeal income (usually about 10 percent) to this objective. With the ALC and the AELC, the LCA funded a food policy staff position at the Washington office of the Lutheran Council in the USA. All three churches also supported ecumenical agencies working on food and hunger concerns at the federal level, including the Interreligious Task Force on U.S. Food Policy and IMPACT.

The LCA's unique contribution in the public-policy arena, however, was at the state level. It pioneered for Lutherans in the creation of coalitions to address state legislation on issues of concern to the church. The first was in Pennsylvania, the state with the largest LCA membership.

"We opened an office in Harrisburg, the capital, in September of 1978," recalls Kay Dowhower, the first director of the

Pennsylvania Lutheran Coalition on Public Policy. "I remember that one of the first things we supported was legislation to allow food that was outdated but perfectly useable to be contributed by grocery stores to local food pantries."

Within about three years, the LCA had launched state coalitions in a dozen or more capitals. They continue as part of the ELCA's ministry today in 18 states.[2] Funding for these advocacy efforts included regular LCA benevolence dollars, though a high percentage of their support came from hunger money. Dowhower recalls:

> We kept careful audits on the percentage of work that was hunger-related, and used hunger funds in that proportion for each state. Of course, there was always debate about which legislative items could be considered hunger-related. Advocacy was new to us, but so was a broad understanding of what really creates hunger. Many of our members thought alleviating hunger meant giving people bags of rice. Basically we said that, in the U.S., hunger is directly tied to such things as poverty and jobs and health care and help to families led by single-parent mothers.

Jim Addington, who directs the ELCA Lutheran Coalition for Public Policy in Minnesota, notes that when the churches speak to government "we will sometimes make mistakes. But it is so important that we be present in state capitols to speak up for poor and marginalized people. Our very presence says a great deal."

It was a big joy, Dowhower says, to be part of starting something completely new for the LCA, and to see it continue in the ELCA. But Dowhower, who now directs the Lutheran Office for Governmental Affairs (LOGA) in Washington, D.C.,[3] regrets that "it's so hard for Lutherans in this country to become serious about public policy work. Even on matters of human need which nearly all church members consider important, such as fighting hunger, we still have lots of skepticism about politics being any part of the solution."

An Office in Washington

At the federal level, U.S. Lutherans have had their own office in Washington dealing specifically with international hunger and development. Opened in the spring of 1975 as a cooperative operation of Lutheran World Relief and Church World Service, it is now known as the Office on Development Policy. From 1975 until 1989, Larry Minear served as its director.

"The office really emerged out of the momentum generated by the United Nations Food Conference in Rome in November of 1974," says Minear. "A major issue at the time was the fragility of world grain reserves and the vulnerability of countries that could not compete in the world market. After the Soviet wheat sale of 1973, it was recognized that there had to be greater protection in times of shortage if food aid was to be a reliable vehicle for relief and development in the poorest nations."

Minear notes that the churches and Bread for the World played a major role in establishing a U.S. grain reserve during the late 1970s. "But we have moved a long way in 15 years from concern with food aid to concern with the actual structures of poverty in the South," he says. "The churches grew in sophistication from matters of food to matters of debt and trade. For our church agencies, such as LWR and CWS, a deepening understanding of the issues has meant progressing in our advocacy work from food aid to food-for-work to grassroots development and now even to peace and reconciliation efforts."

Churches and Credibility

Testimony presented to Congressional committees by the church agencies "always represents more than the views of someone based in Washington," Minear says. The LWR public-policy advocacy, Minear points out, emerges from "regular discussion and decision by the LWR board of directors, following a review of the issues and the options. Board ownership and accountability are essential. And, through ecumenical collegiality, a more solid product results than any one church alone could have produced."

Such testimony is prepared also "in close dialogue with overseas partner organizations and the grassroots constituencies they serve," notes Kathryn Wolford of LWR. "These are people whose lives are often directly impacted by the policies of the U.S. government and multilateral agencies such as the World

Bank and the International Monetary Fund. Our direct links to such people are crucial to our advocacy credibility."

The current director of the LWR/CWS Office on Development Policy, Carol Capps, says the need in the mid-1990s is "complete reform of U.S. foreign assistance. Our basic foreign-aid legislation was adopted in 1961, when Cold War security concerns were primary. We now seek a total overhaul, marked by several core elements: sustainable development as a priority, protection of human rights, local groups always involved in planning and carrying out projects, and attention to the role of women." The LWR/CWS office advocates that these criteria be extended to all U.S. aid, including that moving through such multilateral agencies as the World Bank.

Minear points out that other lobbying groups tend to come and go on the hunger agenda, but not the churches. "In advocating for hungry people, it's the churches that have become the long-distance runners," he says. "From the seventies to the present—that's a marathon! Further, as advocates who have a broad grassroots constituency, both at home and overseas, the churches stand virtually alone."

Spiritual Leaders and Poor People

Through its own office (LOGA—Lutheran Office for Governmental Affairs), the ELCA is also represented in Washington on hunger concerns. The ELCA predecessor churches used hunger funds to maintain a Washington staff position on food policy, and the ELCA continues that practice. Kathleen Daugherty occupied that position during the years prior to the ELCA's formation, from 1980 to 1987. "Those Lutheran denominations had developed a solid social policy base, grounded in Scripture," Daugherty recalls. "That gave us enormous strength to work on a variety of issues, from domestic food programs to farm policy to international trade."[4]

The director of LOGA from 1977 to 1987, Charles Bergstrom, says he recognizes that church statements on public policy "aren't Holy Writ. But silence by the church in the face of injustice is never an answer."

And Bergstrom is pleased that the churches he represented asked LOGA to speak regularly on behalf of poor and hungry people. Too often, he feels, religious groups speak in Washington only to protect their own institutional self-interest. Bergstrom recalls a response he had from Rep. Charles Rangel (D-NY) after he had testified on behalf of the three ELCA predecessor churches in June 1985. Presented to the Subcommittee on Select Revenue Measures of the House Committee on Ways and Means, the testimony outlined the impact which certain tax-reform proposals would have on poor people. When Bergstrom completed his statement, Rangel, who chaired the subcommittee, said:

> I am indeed moved by your testimony. I have seen a lot of religious leaders here in the last couple of months. I have heard about parsonages being exempted from taxes. I have heard a great deal about how we handle contributions to the church. It is unique in this committee to hear spiritual leaders talking about the poor.[5]

And Some Strongly Disagree

But not all Lutherans would share Representative Rangel's enthusiasm—in 1985 or a decade later—about church agencies speaking on behalf of poor and hungry people to the centers of political power. Those who criticize the practice have raised three basic concerns. Such policy statements, they argue, (1) usually do not represent the views of most church members, (2) often go beyond the church's arena of competence, and (3) are a distraction from the church's central task, the proclamation of the gospel.

In the 1980s, Lutheran Pastor Richard John Neuhaus emerged as one of the most vocal critics of churchly speaking on public policy, particularly regarding hunger and poverty. A product of the LCMS, as are Simon and Beckmann, Neuhaus was not opposed to all political activism by Lutherans. An outspoken opponent of U.S. policy in Southeast Asia, he had co-founded Clergy and Laity Concerned About Vietnam in the late sixties. Neuhaus was an early supporter and longtime board member of Bread for the World. But he drew a sharp distinction between political action by individual Christians and the corporate taking of policy positions by church bodies. He supported

the former, thus finding the BFW approach congenial at least in
the movement's early years. He opposed the latter in very strong
language. Neuhaus also felt that people of biblical faith tend to
get tied to policy options that are too specific:

> We do not have a word from the Lord on whether the hungry
> children of the poor should be fed through a food stamp
> program or through a guaranteed annual income. We do
> have a word from the Lord against a system that allows them
> to go hungry.[6]

Neuhaus left Lutheranism in the fall of 1990 and is today
a Roman Catholic priest. Throughout the eighties, he was incessant in his criticism of the use of hunger funds by the ALC,
AELC, and LCA, and then the ELCA, for policy advocacy. A
frequent Neuhaus charge was that hunger staff persons were
representing positions which their denominations had not offi-
cially adopted. Vern Cronmiller, who worked with the hunger
appeals of both the LCA and the ELCA, was one who tried to
communicate regularly with Neuhaus, beseeching him to strive
for factual accuracy. Cronmiller recalls how he felt about the
Neuhaus criticism:

> I believe it is proper to use a portion of hunger dollars for
> changing the situation of hungry people through political
> advocacy by the church. I also feel the critique made by
> Neuhaus and others has to be taken seriously: there must
> always be evidence of support within the membership for
> what the church advocates. My chief problem with the Neu-
> haus attack was its arrogant style and its inaccuracies.

Hunger Politics in the ALC

In the 1980s, the ALC had its own internal debate on politics
and hunger. Among ALC leaders, there was little argument
about the thesis that combating hunger requires political
changes, meaning actions by governments in both the developing countries and the Northern nations. Nor was there much
challenging of the need for Lutherans as citizens to become
vocal advocates with elected officials for constructive policies in

the effort to alleviate hunger. Indeed, as we have seen, the ALC was among the earliest and strongest supporters of Bread for the World, the movement among Christians as citizens to influence federal policy on hunger.

The ALC debate focused rather on the question Neuhaus was raising: Could the ALC Hunger Program itself take sides on particular public policy questions, thus committing the denomination to specific stances in the absence of clear ALC positions? In other words, was it proper to use hunger dollars in an attempt to influence the political thinking of either government officials or ALC members?

At its 1974 birth and during its first two years, the ALC Hunger Program spent nothing on education and public policy work. After 1976, such spending typically ranged from 4% to 7% of each year's receipts, and less than half of that could really be called "political advocacy." At virtually every meeting of the Church Council, the ALC's governing body between its biennial conventions, the question was revived: "Could any hunger dollars at all be used for work in the political realm?"

ALC Presiding Bishop David W. Preus consistently took the position that no hunger money should be used for advocacy that seeks to influence political decisions. Such advocacy should be a part of the ALC's work, he believed, but only when the church had taken a position through structures designated for that purpose, and then using only regular benevolence dollars, not hunger gifts, to carry out the work. Bishop Preus wrote that church members might not support a hunger appeal "if a significant portion of the money is used to advocate political positions with which they disagree."

Also on the Church Council were persons who argued strongly for Hunger Program involvement in political advocacy; among the most vocal was Dr. Jerrold Johnson, a family physician in Whitefish, Montana. In the end, both the Council and General Conventions continued to endorse using a percentage of ALC hunger receipts—though a very slim one—for advocacy.

The issue reached a well-publicized climax in early 1982. Hunger Program Director George Johnson had invited representatives of the 19 ALC districts to take part in a two-week visit to study the causes of hunger in Central America. Upon returning, the group issued a statement which was highly critical of

U.S. government policy in Central America. Bishop Preus found the group's statement "too one-sided, too sweeping in generalizations, and tending to polarize the church." He said it could not be disseminated by the national offices because it would appear to be speaking for the ALC.

Bishop Preus later met with George Johnson and about a dozen of the travelers. The outcome was agreement that the group's statement and a video made during their visit would state clearly that both represented only the travelers' views. At a Church Council meeting a few months later, it was made explicit that ALC corporate advocacy must be based on decisions made by representative, elected bodies of the church.

The Biggest Debate

The LCMS has traditionally not expressed policy positions to government on hunger and poverty. Synod representatives have welcomed such expressions, however, through inter-Lutheran vehicles in which LCMS participates. "I rejoice in the fact that statements on public policy can be made through both Lutheran World Relief and Lutheran Immigration and Refugee Service," says Al Senske, director of LCMS World Relief.

It may well be that the individualized approach offered by Bread for the World is attractive to Lutherans precisely because it does not require the church as an institution to be directly involved in advocacy. That would help to explain the excitement about BFW shared by such varied figures as Richard Neuhaus and ALC Bishop Preus.

But does the church wish to say that only individual Christians, never the people of God collectively, should speak on public questions? (Bishop Preus did not take such a position, but Richard Neuhaus seemed to be saying essentially that in his latter Lutheran years.) It's a question Lutherans and other people of biblical faith will continue to debate. It may be the biggest continuing debate about the use of hunger dollars.[7]

Perhaps Lutherans will not be able to resolve it. Robert Marshall, longtime board president of Lutheran World Relief and a biblical scholar, has always strongly supported the church's advocacy role. Reflecting on the U.S. Lutheran uncertainty about the public-policy arena, Marshall says:

> We Lutherans are skilled at showing compassion to hurting people. We also know how to serve as chaplain to the existing

system. But we're skeptical about being prophetic. Lutheranism was born in an authoritarian society; thus, we understand being chaplains to princes and elites. But where every citizen is to govern, as in a modern democracy, then we Lutherans seem unsure about our role. More and more we're realizing that our citizenship needs guidance from Christian faith as we learn and work together through the church.

There will continue to be disagreement about how Christians should behave in the public realm on behalf of poor and hungry people. But perhaps all can agree with Art Simon's conclusion: "The biggest mistake of all is to take no risks for others. . . . We are free to fail. We are not free to do nothing."[8]

For Discussion

1. Read and discuss Psalm 72, especially verses 1-4 and 12-14. What characterizes the rule of a godly king? In a contemporary democratic system, who is "the king"?

2. Martin Luther, in his Large Catechism commentary on the Fourth Petition of the Lord's Prayer, offers a similar view of the responsibility of the "upright prince" when he writes: "It would be fitting if the coat-of-arms of every upright prince were emblazoned with a loaf of bread instead of a lion or if a loaf of bread were stamped on coins, to remind both princes and subjects that through [government] we enjoy protection and peace and that without [it] we could not have the steady blessing of daily bread." How do you feel about that role for government? Where do you see that role in your nation's present governance system?

3. Discuss the reluctance among Lutherans to support church involvement in political policy work. Why do many of us have, as Kay Dowhower suggests, "skepticism about politics being any part of the solution" to hunger? How does the group respond to the Marshall and Simon comments at the chapter's close?

4. Ask a pair of group members to role-play the case for believers acting as individuals in the public-policy arena. Ask a second pair to make the case for the church corporately to be involved in advocacy. Encourage all members to share their feelings about the two arenas.

END NOTES

1. Robert Stackel, LCA appeal director, 1974-80, recalls that "promoting Bread for the World memberships among LCA people, I'm afraid, was not a priority for us in the 1970s."

2. ELCA advocacy offices are in the capitals of Arizona, California, Colorado, Delaware, Illinois, Iowa, Maryland, Michigan, Minnesota, Nebraska, Nevada, New Jersey, New Mexico, New York, Oregon, Pennsylvania, Washington, and Wisconsin. Collectively, about 30% of their financial support is from hunger funds.

3. The ELCA also maintains a Lutheran Office for World Community at the United Nations in New York; it serves as the Lutheran World Federation's chief representative at the U.N. The LCMS is represented on hunger/development policy through the LWR/CWS office in Washington.

4. ELCA predecessor bodies were also active in the Washington-based Interreligious Task Force on U.S. Food Policy, formed in 1974. In the 1980s it became Interfaith Action and, in the early nineties, merged with IMPACT to create Interfaith IMPACT for Justice and Peace. The ELCA continues to support this agency, whose agenda includes a broad range of policy issues.

5. Representative Rangel's comment suggests a distinction that is often drawn when church groups seek to influence government decision makers. The distinction is between *lobbying*, in which a church institution's own self-interest is being pursued, and *advocacy*, in which justice is being sought for those who are relatively voiceless/powerless or on behalf of the whole human family.

6. Neuhaus, *Christian Faith and Public Policy: Thinking and Acting in the Courage of Uncertainty* (Minneapolis: Augsburg, 1977), p. 52.

7. About 4% of ELCA hunger giving—roughly $500,000 annually—is presently designated for hunger advocacy work, chiefly through the Washington, D.C.; New York; and 18 state offices. Hunger advocacy funds also provide grants to Bread for the World, Interfaith IMPACT, and other ecumenical advocacy organizations. LCMS World Relief responds to Bread for the World funding requests on a project-by-project basis.

8. Simon, *Christian Faith and Public Policy: No Grounds for Divorce* (Grand Rapids: Eerdmans, 1987), p. viii.

PEOPLE WHO ARE MAKING A DIFFERENCE

For tens of thousands of U.S. Lutherans, hunger ministry in the past couple of decades has become their most visible continuing response to the gospel. They would say God has called them to put their faith into deeds by addressing the needs of people who are poor and hungry.

Of these many servants of God, you will meet just a few in this chapter. You will hear in their own words how Christian faith and loving action have come together. You will see that they are ordinary people who have been empowered by God's Spirit to do extraordinary things. (They are pictured in the book's photo section.) You will learn about the church's role as inspirer, equipper, and meaning-giver for their service. Meet, then, several people who are making a difference in the struggle against poverty and hunger.

> *"Roadrunner for Christ" is a ministry born out of love and faith, following Christ's command to feed, clothe, and care for those in need. "Roadrunner" comes from my Indian name, "Hospoamana." I'll continue to help poor people meet their physical needs, but more important is that we plant the seed of the gospel.*
>
> —Jeanne Cordova

Alberto Rodriguez: Nebraska

In Nebraska, Alberto Rodriguez, a former migrant worker, has devoted himself to hunger ministries for the past 25 years. Al has become known in the Omaha area as a kind of omnipresent ombudsperson for those who are left out of mainstream society. Part of a Mexican-American family from Texas, he was traveling through Omaha in 1968 when his car broke down. He's been there ever since.

Al makes his living as a custodian, working in recent years for Omaha public schools. His other job, for which he is not paid, has been made up of a long list of volunteer activities, "trying to create vehicles that will provide solutions for those who are not able to look after themselves." He helped to create the Omaha Lutheran Pantry. He was a cofounder of the Chicano Awareness Center and of a bilingual Head Start program. He works with the Latino Forum of Nebraska. In 1993 he successfully completed a five-year struggle to get Nebraska to provide driver's manuals in Spanish and Vietnamese.

In his paid job, at school, "I do more than sweep rooms," Al says. He often translates Spanish for teachers and counselors, interprets at parent conferences, and helps educators write letters to Spanish-speaking parents. As vice president of his Service Employees International Union Local 226, Al has made job safety in local meat-packing plants a priority. His major project in the mid-1990s is the attempt to create a multi-ethnic marketplace in south Omaha. For that effort's nonprofit Mercado Corporation, which seeks to generate jobs for low-income persons, he serves as volunteer president.

A longtime member of Christ the King Lutheran congregation (ELCA) in Omaha, Al credits the church with providing both material resources and theological inspiration to support his activism. "Our national church has played a major role in supporting the community projects I'm involved with," he says. "At the synod level, bishops, pastors, and lay folks have written letters and testified before governors and legislators for political purposes that benefited those who are less fortunate. And congregations locally have provided resources to assist needy people of all sorts." Contributors to the Mercado project include Lord of Love Lutheran Church, Lutheran Metropolitan Ministries, and Aid Association for Lutherans.

Al believes God is calling him to make a difference. God's plan, he says, "is that if we share the earth's resources responsibly, the human race will flourish. That scenario is not currently the case. I was put on this earth for a purpose. That's why I believe my participation in the community process is making a difference—for me and for those around me."

Donald Nelsen: Kansas

"I believe the Lord began to lay on my heart the plight of the hungry during my tour of duty in Vietnam," says Donald Nelsen of Copeland, Kansas. "Seeing hungry children feverishly rummaging through garbage for any scrap of food opened my eyes to the horrors of poverty."

Don and his wife, Carolyn, are farmers. They believed God was calling them to help feed the world through the occupation of farming. "But deep down inside," Don says, "we felt the Lord was preparing us for a more personal involvement in feeding the hungry. I was in fervent prayer over this for 15 years." Don says his praying received an answer in 1984, when a young vicar was sent by the LCMS Kansas District to nearby Garden City. Vicar David Loza's assignment: survey southwest Kansas to determine the feasibility of launching ministry among Hispanic people there. Through home visits, Vicar Loza soon discovered there were families who did not have enough to eat. When the Nelsens heard that, they organized a collection of food for 21 families at Thanksgiving time, 1984.

The project grew. "Being farmers," he says, "we took wheat and corn we had grown to the mill to be ground into flour and cornmeal. We took hogs to slaughter to provide sausage. We contacted pinto bean and potato producers and arranged bulk purchases." By 1989, the venture had expanded to the point that institutional help was needed. He involved a number of area agencies, including Emmaus House, Mexican-American Ministries, Harvest America, Salvation Army, Social and Rehabilitation Services, and Family Crisis.

The effort provides basic staples with a long shelf life—such as beans, flour, potatoes, rice—to supplement a family's diet for several months. The food distribution happens in the late fall, usually the first weekend in December. Contributions come from individuals, businesses, churches, and community service organizations. From 21 families served in 1984, the project has grown so that nearly 1,000 families were assisted in December 1993, when 130,000 pounds of food was shared.

"In 1990, when area farms were hit by a devastating hail storm, we turned to LCMS World Relief for financial help," Don reports. "We received a $7,000 grant that year and a $9,900 grant in 1991." But most of the contributions continue to come from producers and businesses in Kansas and adjacent states. All labor is provided by volunteers—it exceeded 800 person-hours in 1993. Jerry Thomas of Emporia, who owns a moving van company, has been especially helpful in transporting commodities for distribution in southwest Kansas. "Feed the Children in Oklahoma City is also a major contributor," Don says.

There have been disappointments. "We have encountered the attitude that the poor are lazy and undeserving of help," Don says. "But we believe the Lord lays the responsibility of caring for the needy on the people of God. Isaiah 58 says 'to share your food with the hungry' is 'fasting acceptable to God.' We have not been successful in gaining support for our food distribution from the Lutheran congregations in southwest Kansas, though some Lutheran individuals have made generous contributions of time and funding. And we are very grateful for substantial support from LCMS World Relief."

In 1989, the Nelsens began distributing Bibles—in Spanish, Vietnamese, and English—along with food. Funds for the Bibles have come from a local branch of Aid Association for Lutherans and individual donors. The Nelsens have also worked closely during the past several years with La Santa Cruz Lutheran Mission in Garden City, which serves Spanish-speaking people with a Word and Sacrament ministry.

Carolyn Nelsen suffered paralyzing injury through an auto accident in 1986. "It has permanently altered our lives," Don says. "But despite hardships, the Lord has always provided the means to continue feeding the hungry. We know God's grace saves us and no work on our part can gain salvation. But God didn't save us for our own benefit alone. God intends our salvation to lead to deeds of service which God prepared for us to do even before he created the world."

Dorothy Borge: Montana

Since 1989, Dorothy Borge has been hunger program coordinator for the ELCA Montana Synod. In that role, she seeks "to get congregational hunger contact people appointed to bring hunger/justice issues before their congregations." Her interest in poverty and hunger ministry, however, is not a recent development.

"It seems like I have almost always had a concern for poor and hungry people," Dorothy says. "As a small child in Wisconsin, it was through the church that my world took on its first 'out there' concern. Then, at Luther College in Decorah, Iowa, in the summers of 1967 and 1968, I worked with Upward Bound, a program for high schoolers from low-income families. I've been a member of Bread for the World, I think from its beginning, and am a supporter of Habitat for Humanity as well."

Dorothy credits her 1979 move to the northcentral Montana community of Conrad with deepening her hunger involvement. "I found a mentor in Virginia Dyrud and others in our parish [Golden West and Pondera Valley Lutheran churches]," she says. "For years, they have been faithfully educating, witnessing, and upholding people who are at work helping to alleviate hunger and poverty in our community and around the world."

With colleagues in her congregation and nearby Lutheran parishes, Dorothy has helped to organize the first local CROP Walk for the Hungry, the collection of garden produce and other items for a food pantry, and the donation of wild game for low-income residents. She credits her national church with "continuing my education and involvement. The more I learn of what our ELCA hunger money is doing around the world, the more I'm convinced of the wonderful avenue our church provides to help us in the fight against hunger and injustice."

Dorothy and her husband, Michael, have made hunger a priority throughout their marriage. "Early in our life together, we made a decision to give a percentage of our income each month to hunger concerns. We're thankful that we have been able to continue this." She sees her faith and her commitment to work in hunger ministries as inseparable:

> It is because of my Christian faith that I feel called to use the gifts God has given me—whether as organizer, letter-writer, donor, quilter, encourager, pray-er, or listener. It is

because of my faith that I can repeatedly fail to use those gifts and know that I am forgiven and can start over. I feel that God, through Scripture, is giving a mandate to us all to help the poor and hungry.

Mildred Grady and Norma Marks: Florida

Mildred Grady and Norma Marks are sisters and members of Hope Lutheran Church (LCMS) in Pompano Beach, Florida. They believe God has called them to enlist church resources on behalf of poor and homeless people in their community. Their congregation has been involved with Meals on Wheels food deliveries for more than a decade and has been a distribution center for U.S. government food as well.

But since 1991, Mildred and Norma have coordinated a special ministry in which Hope feeds homeless people at a local day shelter, St. Laurence Chapel. Sponsored by the Episcopal Church, the shelter has ecumenical support. Hope Church provides a hot dinner for up to 100 homeless persons one Sunday each month year-round. It was through Hope's leadership that other area congregations have been drawn into serving, so that all Sundays are now covered.

And, every Tuesday, the children of Hope's elementary school provide sandwiches for people at the shelter. On that day the pastor of Hope, Dwayne C. Hoyer, preaches at the St. Laurence worship service. The Hope children also make 100 place mats every month with biblical words of love.

Hope's meal program began with a Thanksgiving dinner in 1991 that served 300 persons. The tradition continues and the numbers have grown to about 500.

Since 1991, one sister or the other has chaired Hope's social ministry committee, which coordinates the congregation's outreach to people in need. "They understand how to connect the faith to the needs of hurting people through love offerings," says Pastor Hoyer. "They are also good organizers and fine stewards of limited resources."

Pastor Hoyer believes the food programs have been an excellent vehicle for congregational outreach, especially "among our large Haitian community." The effort has been supported by LCMS World Relief grants, by Aid Association for Lutherans, and by local grocery stores, as well as by the congregation itself.

Hope Church "is very committed to this work," Mildred and Norma report. "Our committee feels that God has blessed us richly and that his love can shine through us as we serve others who are in need."

Mary Nelson: Illinois

It was 1965 and David Nelson was moving to an inner-city pastorate on the west side of Chicago. Mary Nelson, his sister, was along "to help my bachelor brother get settled in his new setting. Three days later, the first of the riots of the 1960s erupted. We've been here ever since."

It's been a busy three decades for Mary Nelson. Her commitment to the community has led to her becoming the president of Bethel New Life, Inc., a church-related community development corporation. Located in a low-income, African American community, Bethel New Life is sponsored by Bethel Lutheran Church, a predominately African American ELCA congregation.

Bethel New Life takes a comprehensive approach to community development, including affordable housing, livable wage job creation, holistic health, and empowerment of people. "We are driven by Isaiah 58:9-12," says Mary. "To a people who are faithful to the call of justice, God promises to rebuild the ruined cities." The corporation is literally rebuilding its part of Chicago, by such actions as turning an abandoned school into 26 affordable apartments and a closed hospital into an acute-care facility and housing for the elderly. As Mary observes, it all happened because God gave Bethel Church a vision:

> The congregation knew that, to be the church, we had to be addressing the agony of the community, in partnership with the people of the community. We began with a small vision and have evolved into a holistic response that still has a long way to go. Bethel and the gospel preached there have been the glue to hold us together, the gasoline to keep us going when things seemed so difficult, and the guts to tackle the impossible things.

Members of Bethel are involved in every aspect of Bethel New Life. "But most of all," Mary says, "the congregation is there to remind us of God's vision, to supply hope, and to be a supportive community to pick us up when we are down and disappointed."

Mary's own leadership abilities are no small part of the development corporation's effectiveness. She says she is driven by a strong call from God "to be about justice." Beyond that, Mary believes she is following the legacy left by her mother. When Ruth Youngdahl Nelson, at age 78, was arrested for putting her body in a frail boat in front of a Trident nuclear submarine in Puget Sound, reporters asked her, "Why does an American Mother of the Year break the law?" Ruth Nelson immediately responded, "I do it for the children of the world."

Says Mary Nelson, "What a heritage of faith is mine!"

Jeanne Cordova: Colorado

While Jeanne Cordova lives in Denver, her ministry reaches poor and hungry people not only in Colorado but also in Arizona, New Mexico, Texas, and even across the Mexican border. A member of the Hopi nation, Jeanne has focused her volunteer ministry on "the poorest of the poor, the people who live in cardboard houses and are totally destitute."

She started her work more than 15 years ago, "bringing clothes, medicines, and food to Hopi and Navaho people in New Mexico and to an orphanage in El Sausal, Mexico." Jeanne's congregation, Concordia Lutheran Church (LCMS) in Lakewood, Colorado, "has always supported the work by providing food and clothing for me to take to Mexico and to those in need in the Denver area." Every second or third week, she drives a van loaded with food, clothing, toys, and household goods to locations across the border from El Paso, Texas. Jeanne also collects food and clothing from congregations of several denominations in and around Ogallala and Wallace, Nebraska.

The ministry is called "Roadrunner for Christ," after Jeanne's Hopi name, "Hospoamana." She describes her work as ". . . a ministry born out of love and faith, following Christ's command to feed, clothe, and care for those in need. I'll continue to help poor people meet their physical needs, but more important is that we plant the seed of the gospel."

In 1980, Jeanne launched at Concordia Church a Christmas basket program, which, each Christmas, provides food for at least a week and gifts for more than 100 families "of all sizes and nationalities" in the Denver area. "We also support Jeffco Action Center and the food bank at Cordero de Dios, an LCMS Hispanic congregation in Denver."

In addition to her congregational base, Jeanne has had "great support from the LCMS Rocky Mountain District." A Denver area gleaning project which she helped to organize received a seed-money grant from LCMS World Relief.

"My motivation has always been the belief that the Holy Spirit is leading me to do what God has wanted me to do," Jeanne says. "I thank the Lord that he has chosen me for this work."

Kenneth Peterson: Minnesota

"I was a delegate to the 1974 ALC convention in Detroit when the Hunger Program was launched," says Kenneth Peterson of Tamarack, Minnesota. Ken has been a hunger activist ever since. He recalls being at one of the early meetings in the Midwest "when Art Simon was beginning to make Bread for the World a national movement." He was a participant in the 1975 ALC consultation of farmers on food and hunger concerns and, that same year, organized the first hunger workshop in northern Minnesota.

Ken's general sense of justice was first awakened "in the 1950s, when I was serving in the army in Alabama. One day in Montgomery, I was the first person on a city bus and sat in the back row. The driver looked into the mirror, saw me, stopped the bus, and said, 'The back of the bus is for niggers.' Many of my army buddies bragged how they persecuted, even killed, blacks. I bought Martin Luther King's dream early on."

A dairy farmer most of his life, Ken "once believed that we U.S. farmers had the ability to produce enough food to feed a hungry world. But long ago I learned that what we need is a more just world, allowing people everywhere the opportunity and dignity of feeding themselves." Ken claims that church-sponsored study trips to Central America, Haiti, and the Philippines have sharpened his sensitivity to the realities of the developing world. He is a recognized leader for hunger ministries in his synod and throughout the Upper Midwest region of the ELCA.

Ken has been an advocate not only for poor people overseas, but also for those who are economically distressed in this country, which includes many family farmers. In recent years he has worked part-time as an advocate for farmers in northeast Minnesota through the Extension Service of Carlton County. He continues in farming with a beef cow-calf operation. Ken also has served as secretary of the Minnesota Sustainable Farming Association almost from its beginning in 1990.

"My greatest concern," says Ken, "is that our country does not have a food policy. Every five years we get a farm program which reflects the views of the party in power. But our foreign policy is the true bottom line. The social impact of federal policies on families, communities, and entire nations doesn't get considered."

A member of Bethlehem Lutheran Church in Wright, Minnesota, Ken credits the gospel with moving him to strive for a more just world. For him, the parable of the rich man and Lazarus "is one of the most powerful biblical statements about our lives in relation to the hungry and the poor. I have also learned a great deal from poor people about understanding the grace of God and how to follow Christ," he says.

"I'm grateful to my church," says Ken Peterson, "that it has given me an opportunity for more than 20 years to be one small voice on justice issues for hungry people and for rural America."

For Discussion

1. Read and discuss 1 John 3:16-18. What could it be saying to the people of God in your congregation today?

2. All of those profiled in this chapter credit the church with giving them an awareness of needs in the larger world. Has that been the experience of members of your group? If so, how and when has it happened? If not, what was missing that the people introduced here were privileged to experience?

3. The farmers—Donald and Carolyn Nelsen and Ken Peterson—reached the conclusion that God was calling them to do more about hunger than produce food, though they continued doing that as well. What does the group think of their conclusion? How does God call any of us to service through both our jobs and other avenues?

4. Most of the persons profiled in this chapter report having faced disappointments, among them being rebuffed by other Christians. What are the factors that keep them going, that provide continuing hope?

WHEN WILL IT ALL END?

We conclude with a question: What shape will hunger ministries in these two Lutheran churches assume in the future? Behind that question, of course, is a more basic one: Will hunger and poverty always be part of the human experience, or may we expect a time, prior to God's "new heaven and new earth," when the suffering of material need will no longer plague the lives of people on this planet?

The elimination of hunger is, in my opinion, on the ambitious edge of a modest but attainable measure of justice. There is no guarantee that hunger will be eliminated. It can *be eliminated, just as slavery and tyranny have been eliminated in many places, so we must make every effort toward that end.*

—Arthur Simon

That second question has been around a long time. It's a biblical question and no doubt existed long before there were written Scriptures. Part of the promise to God's people of promise was that "there will, however, be no one in need among you, because the LORD is sure to bless you in the land which the LORD your God is giving you as a possession to occupy" (Deuteronomy 15:4). The rest of the sentence clearly links that promise with God's expectation that the people would keep *their* side of the covenant: you will have "no one in need among you if only you will obey the LORD your God, by diligently observing this entire commandment that I command you today."[1] Later in the fifteenth chapter, the people are told, "Since there will never cease to be some in need on the earth, I therefore command you, 'Open your hand to the poor and needy neighbor in your land' " (Deuteronomy 15:11).

"This entire commandment" in Deuteronomy provides, incidentally, some guidelines that are still helpful in combating poverty today: the call for sharing by those who have more than they need, the provision for periodic redistribution of land, and the recognition that the land must have its rest.

'Always the Poor with You'?

"Since there will never cease to be some in need" reminds us of a word from Jesus. This word is frequently quoted—most often, it seems, by those who wish to make a point other than the one our Lord was making. When some of Jesus' followers scolded the woman who anointed him with costly ointment, arguing that it could have been sold and the money given to poor people, Jesus told them to stop troubling the woman. "She has performed a good service for me. For you always have the poor with you, and you can show kindness to them whenever you wish; but you will not always have me" (Mark 14:6-7).

That reprimand from Jesus seems to be repeated mostly by people who seek the Lord's support for the view that poverty is inevitable and eternal. That being the case, they argue, there's not much we can do to change things. Close examination of Jesus' comments, both here and elsewhere in the Gospels, however, indicates that our Lord is not urging his followers to ignore the needs of poor people. Quite the contrary. The Mark 14 story reveals that those who criticized the woman had indeed captured Jesus' concern for poor people. It also tells us that Jesus was not abandoning that concern ("you can show them kindness whenever you wish"). His main point was a different one: that the woman was doing her loving deed in a unique situation ("she has anointed my body beforehand for its burial").

"When I'm physically no longer with you," Jesus is saying, "there will be plenty of opportunity for my disciples to serve poor people." In no way can those who follow Jesus today quote Mark 14 in order to avoid responsibility for showing love to neighbors. The whole biblical record makes clear that such neighbor-love is what God expects the people of God to be doing.

Nor can we quote Mark 14 to support the argument that God wills poverty to be permanent, any more than we would use the existence of slavery in biblical times to argue that slavery is divinely authorized and inevitable in human society. Just as the institution of slavery has been eliminated as a standard feature of social order in virtually all parts of the world, so also we can envision the elimination of chronic hunger.

Further, most food scientists claim that it *is* possible today for all of the planet's billions of people to have an adequate daily diet. The core problem, they say, is not the earth's producing capacity; it is rather a result of the fact that many people have inequitable and grossly inadequate access to the resources needed for feeding themselves. So equitable distribution of resources is a major issue.

Other observers note that the planet continues to have serious problems with inadequate food production as well. Producing an adequate food supply—in ways that are environmentally sustainable and for a human population that continues to grow—is not a simple challenge.

Yet, for this believer, the conclusion is unavoidable: God has given humankind a world bursting with capacity for creating food ("The earth produces of itself . . ." Mark 4:28), and has entrusted to us the management of this marvelous resource and the fair distribution of what it can produce so that all may be fed.

'No Child Shall Go to Bed Hungry'

Political leaders, on occasion, will voice the expectation that hunger can be ended. One of the more famous such statements was that of U.S. Secretary of State Henry Kissinger at the World Food Conference in Rome, November 1974. At that moment, Kissinger said, the peoples of the earth should pledge to achieve within a decade the goal of "no child going to bed hungry anywhere in the world."

That worthy goal was, obviously, not achieved by 1984, not by 1994, and most likely will not be a reality by 2004. There are millions in our day, children and adults, who face serious food insecurity. Not all are in the developing countries. Northern industrialized nations, such as the United States and

Canada, and the lands of the former Soviet Union and its eastern European satellites also have citizens who are poor. Without social safety nets, the poor of these nations would also be staring at starvation.

And yet, there are large parts of the globe in which hunger *has* been eliminated. This fact leads to hope that it can one day be ended everywhere. Pastor Arthur Simon, the founder of Bread for the World, does not take a utopian view of human nature and social change. Holding a Lutheran's traditional view of the pervasiveness of human sin, he writes, "The world is incurably resistant to anything like the advent of complete justice and peace. This side of the Resurrection, a modest measure of justice may be the best we can hope to achieve." Indeed, Simon shares a view held by Martin Luther, that the world is easily made worse but improved only with great difficulty.

Yet, Simon is persuaded that "the elimination of hunger is on the ambitious edge of a modest but attainable measure of justice. There is no guarantee that hunger will be eliminated. It *can* be eliminated, just as slavery and tyranny have been eliminated in many places, so we must make every effort toward that end."[2]

With Us for a While Yet

There is no reason to believe that hunger will be ended soon, says Simon, nor even that modest gains against it will come easily. Thus, it is a safe guess that hunger will continue to be a global ailment well into the 21st century. And that means there will be a continuing need for the churches to have mechanisms like LCMS World Relief and ELCA World Hunger. What was seen as temporary response, when birthed decades ago, is now perceived by us as permanent. What then can we say about the future of this effort?

It will be useful to look at some trends and to hear some reflections from those who have worked closely with hunger ministries. First, the monetary data: members of the ELCA (or its predecessors) and the LCMS during the 1984-93 decade have given an average of $17,000,000 annually for world hunger/world relief. That's slightly more than $2 a year for each of these churches' nearly 8,000,000 baptized members—a pittance

individually, yet substantial when enough individuals are
involved. Annual totals in that decade ranged from a low of
$14,300,000 to a high of $20,050,000. The peak came in 1985,
when media attention to famine in the Horn of Africa was
intense.[3]

It is noteworthy that hunger giving in ELCA predecessor
churches, on a per-member basis, showed sizeable variations. It
was regularly 25% to 30% higher in the LCA than in the ALC
or AELC, almost certainly a reflection of the fact that the latter
two churches never had full-time staff working solely on fund-
raising. "We proposed that staffing be added for the appeal,"
George Johnson recalls, "but were unable to get that approved."

Since 1987, the relief/hunger income trend for both
ELCA and LCMS has been modestly upward. Thus, there is reason to hope that the two churches' national hunger/relief
receipts will continue in the annual range of $16 to $20 million.
The ELCA's experience of a 7.7% drop between 1992 and 1993
was quite possibly caused by a shift from the Hunger Appeal to
domestic disaster giving, which is not counted with that church's
hunger income. With an unusually large response to Midwest
flooding, 1993 ELCA domestic disaster income was up by more
than $1,000,000 over the previous year; hunger income was
down by about $950,000.

The two churches raise relief/hunger funds in somewhat
differing ways. Slightly more than half of LCMS World Relief
income is given directly by individual donors who receive mail-
ings on a regular basis. In ELCA, close to 90% of the funds are
remitted by congregations. About 75% of local churches in
ELCA conduct hunger appeal activities; most do so at particular
seasons but some of them conduct hunger fund-raising throughout the year. "We are intensely grateful for our congregational
fund-raisers who are, of course, volunteers," says John Halvorson, ELCA Hunger Program coordinator. "Because of them, we
are able to keep our fund-raising costs down to 4%."

Challenging Trends

One practice that seems to be growing could increase the administrative costs for both churches, however. It reflects the desire
of donors, whether individuals or congregations, to designate

their gift for a particular part of the world or kind of activity. In its extreme, a designation could be for a specific overseas project of LWR, for example, which a donor happens to like. Or it could be a request that a gift be limited to work in an inner-city community of the United States, or that none of it be used for advocacy purposes.

"We try to honor anyone's request for designating a gift," says Al Senske of LCMS World Relief. "But we also tell folks that the less specific they are the more flexible and efficient we can be in putting every dollar of their gift to work on behalf of hungry people." Roger Livdahl, Hunger Appeal director for ELCA, concurs: "If we move very far in the direction of accommodating the desire of people to designate, we will not be able to maintain our low administrative overhead."

Some observers argue that, if congregations and individuals *were* encouraged to designate for specific purposes, total world relief/world hunger giving would increase substantially. A well-designed testing of that thesis would be most instructive for what will surely be a continuing debate.

Another trend in the psychology of giving causes some concern. It is the growing preference for giving to a venture that is close to home, where the donor can see direct results. Such a desire does not resound positively for church programs whose reach is national and international. "Obviously, we need to do both," says Halvorson. "Some of the neighbors God gives us to love are surely in our own front yard. But some are half-way around the globe and we will likely never see them or the efforts to work with them which our gifts support."

The world hunger/world relief appeals clearly face increased competition for dollars. Both individuals—via incessant direct-mail and television bombardment—and congregations are hearing from a growing number of good causes, all fitting under the general category of help to poor people. As these requests increase, Lutheran people do respond, both individually and through their congregations. Thus, unless the total number of hunger dollars given by Lutherans can be expanded, both LCMS World Relief and ELCA World Hunger face the prospect of decline in resources available.

A dominant factor affecting income for world relief/world hunger is the role played by communication media. It has been a fact of life for the appeals from the outset that secular media attention (or neglect) has powerful influence on the giving of church people.

"On the one hand, it is satisfying to see the responsiveness of our members to crises, when they hear about them," says Robert Marshall, longtime president of LWR. "On the other hand, it is disappointing to learn how many church members respond *only* to what they hear from the public media. Journalists are notorious for losing interest in a very short time, but it is simply a fact that many of the needs will be continuing for a very long time."

What Shall We Call It?

One question for the future is what terminology Lutherans should use for their work in "world relief/world hunger" (a concern discussed briefly in this book's Introduction). The question gets raised regarding the programs of both churches, but thus far there has not been much movement toward different language.

"Personally, I'd like to see a study of a possible name change, though there is little agitation for a change in the Synod," says Al Senske of LCMS World Relief. That unit is under the umbrella of the LCMS Board for Human Care Ministries, and "human care" is sometimes used as a broader indication of the "world relief" agenda.

In ELCA circles, "hunger" is sometimes considered too limiting for the work supported by the Hunger Program. "Some think our present name is archaic, and perhaps even deceptive," says John Halvorson. "I'm not convinced we should change it, but I do think there needs to be serious conversation about it.

"We're also aware that much of the ELCA continues to have a profound fondness for their church's Hunger Program," Halvorson observes. "That makes us hesitant about any move to give this ministry a changed identity."

The name question surfaces with Lutheran World Relief as well, for two primary reasons. One is the fact that "relief" is much too narrow a term for the work LWR is now supporting. The second reason is that U.S. Lutherans regularly (and understandably) confuse LWR with Lutheran World Federation, the international association of Lutheran churches.

Name changes for institutions face at least two problems, of course. One is the inevitable loss of identification and momentum, at least for some years, while a constituency learns the new name. The second problem is coming up with a name that is better than what now exists. There can be broad agreement that a given name is inadequate, but very little agreement on what other name might be an improvement. That seems to be the situation with regard to finding acceptable replacements for "world hunger" or "world relief."[4]

Hurry Up but Be Patient!

A concluding word is about perseverance for the long haul. With poverty and hunger likely to be part of the human experience for the rest of our lives, it is proper to conclude that loving the hungry neighbor will continue to be part of the job description for God's people. But how do such people avoid burnout? Can we immunize ourselves against what is often called "compassion fatigue"?

We know the task is urgent. People who hunger today need help today; they cannot wait. It is obscene for the well-fed to say, "Be patient; one day God will give you a better deal, a fuller meal." Christians know that God is urgent about identifying with the needs of poor people, oppressed people, indeed with all of the human lot. That's what the cross means. It is the sign of God's total commitment to our reality.

But the hunger-ministry task also demands patient endurance for the long term. Our God is a patient God. Surely God was patient with the children of Israel. God spent 40 years trying to teach Israel essentially one thing: to place absolute trust in God. What staggering patience on God's part! Kosuke Koyama, a Japanese Christian theologian, says God "is a three-mile-per-hour God," because that's how fast the average person walks. It is thus God's pace in accompanying us during our wanderings in the wilderness.

Perhaps we should not think in years or in decades about the hunger struggle, but in 40-year spans. Biblically, 40 means a long period, a time in which a people learn endurance through suffering and come out tested, prepared for mission. Literally, 40 years is half a lifetime. But symbolically and poetically it may be more than a literal 480 months. It may be a very long time indeed, as long as the present age continues.

We are called to patience, we who are not content with three miles per hour for anything, not content with even 65 miles per hour on the surface, or 10 times that in the air. Our calling is to settle in for the rest of our lifetimes, to nibble away at the challenge a bit at a time, to think beyond one four-year presidential administration or one 10-year United Nations development decade. We are to be urgent, but also patient.

The Letter of James reminds us to be patient as the farmer is patient waiting for the crop and as God's prophets are patient when speaking God's message to an unresponsive people (James 5:7-11). The prophet imagery has dangers for us, because prophets are usually distanced from the people and viewed as carrying a special awareness of God's intentions. But prophetic impulses are what hunger ministries are all about: critique of what is and envisioning of what God wants there to be.

Finally, St. Paul asks that we "not grow weary in well-doing" (Galatians 6:9 RSV). We can pray that we will not, and can include in that prayer: "God, let us not become self-righteous in our well-doing. And let us not lose either our passion or our patience for well-doing."

For Discussion

1. Read Revelation 7:16-17. When do members of the group think the promises of this passage will be fulfilled? In the meantime, are there ways we can be bringing closer their fulfillment?

2. "Give us this day our daily bread"—in praying it, how much do we Christians focus basically on ourselves and our loved ones? How can our praying include bread for our neighbors, near and far?

3. What creative alternatives to the names "Lutheran World Relief," "LCMS World Relief," and "ELCA World Hunger" can the group suggest? All three entities would welcome suggestions— see Appendix B for addresses.

4. How can people working to alleviate poverty and hunger avoid burnout? What gifts can a community of faith provide for the task? How does your congregation work at energizing members for human-care ministries?

END NOTES

1. The passage is echoed by the fourth stanza of the hymn "Praise and Thanksgiving" (*Lutheran Book of Worship*, No. 409), in these words: "Where all obey you, No one will hunger." The hymn also appears in *Lutheran Worship* (No. 403), but the "Where all obey you" stanza, unfortunately, is omitted.

2. Simon, *Christian Faith and Public Policy: No Grounds for Divorce* (Grand Rapids, Michigan: Eerdmans, 1987, pp. 93-95).

3. The all-time high for LCMS world relief income, which includes response to U.S. disasters, came in the fiscal year ending June 30, 1993. Major giving for domestic disaster relief was a part of that year's total. For complete 1970-93 data, see Appendix A.

4. In the late 1970s, the ALC considered "Human Development Appeal" as a new name for its hunger appeal. But when planning began for what became the ELCA, name-change discussions were dropped. See also this chapter's Discussion Item 3.

WORLD RELIEF AND HUNGER APPEAL INCOME

for U.S. Lutheran denominations, 1970-93 (in thousands)

Year	LCMS*	AELC	ALC	LCA	ELCA	Total
1970	650					650
1971	750					750
1972	600					600
1973	750					750
1974	900		2,039	1,876	3,915♦	4,815
1975	1,500		1,602	4,698	6,300♦	7,800
1976	1,900		1,119	3,232	4,351♦	6,251
1977	1,900	50★	1,044	2,626	3,720♦	5,620
1978	2,100	50★	1,065	2,212	3,327♦	5,427
1979	1,600	50★	1,950	3,231	5,231♦	6,831
1980	1,500	50★	2,093	4,019	6,162♦	7,662
1981	1,650	62	2,510	5,360	7,932♦	9,582
1982	2,000	60★	2,914	5,689	8,663♦	10,663
1983	2,350	63	3,133	6,031	9,227♦	11,577
1984	2,850	140★	5,853	8,490	14,483♦	17,333
1985	5,860	136	5,283	8,773	14,192♦	20,052
1986	4,760	120★	4,300	6,648■	11,068♦	15,828
1987	3,970	120★	3,768	6,436■	10,324♦	14,294
1988	3,930				10,695	14,625
1989	4,310				10,748	15,058
1990	4,920				11,653	16,573
1991	4,670				12,017	16,687
1992	4,290				12,297	16,587
1993	6,900				11,350	18,250
	66,610	901	38,673	69,321	68,760	244,265

* LCMS figures from early 1980s onward are for fiscal years ending 30 June of year indicated. LCMS totals for the 1970s are estimates.

★ AELC figures for these years are estimates.

■ Beginning with 1986, income from LCA's former synods in Canada went to ELC in Canada.

♦ Totals for ELCA predecessor bodies.

LCMS totals include emergency disaster response gifts; totals for other churches do not.

Totals for LCMS do not include bequest income; totals for other churches do include bequest income.

ORGANIZATIONS

Lutheran-sponsored Organizations

LCMS WORLD RELIEF
1333 South Kirkwood Road
St. Louis, MO 63122-7295
314/965-9000

ELCA WORLD HUNGER APPEAL/PROGRAM
8765 West Higgins Road
Chicago, IL 60631
800/638-3522

LUTHERAN WORLD RELIEF
390 Park Avenue South
New York, NY 10016-8803
212/532-6350

LUTHERAN WORLD FEDERATION
Departments of World Service and Mission and Development
150 Route de Ferney, Box 2100
CH 1211 Geneva 2 Switzerland
001 41 (22) 791-6111

LUTHERAN OFFICE FOR GOVERNMENTAL AFFAIRS,
  ELCA
122 C Street NW, Suite 125
Washington, DC 20001
202/783-7507

LUTHERAN OFFICE FOR WORLD COMMUNITY, ELCA
(main representative for Lutheran World Federation at United
Nations headquarters)
777 United Nations Plaza
New York, NY 10017
212/808-5360

OFFICE ON DEVELOPMENT POLICY, LWR/CWS
110 Maryland Avenue NE, Box 45
Washington, DC 20002-5694
202/543-6336

LUTHERAN IMMIGRATION AND REFUGEE SERVICE
390 Park Avenue South
New York, NY 10016-8803
212/532-6350

Ecumenical Organizations

ALTERNATIVES
BOX 429, 5263 Bouldercrest Road
Ellenwood, GA 30049
404/961-0102

BREAD FOR THE WORLD
1100 Wayne Avenue, Suite 1000
Silver Spring, MD 20910
301/608-2400

CHURCH WORLD SERVICE AND WITNESS
475 Riverside Drive
New York, NY 10115
212/870-2200

INTERFAITH IMPACT
100 Maryland Avenue NE
Washington, DC 20002
202/543-2800

THE MODES OF RELIEF, DEVELOPMENT, SYSTEMIC CHANGE

All columns are valid responses, given the starting point. In some situations—and for many persons and agencies—there is a progression from I to II to III.
                                                                    —*Charles P. Lutz*

	I: RELIEF	II: DEVELOPMENT	III: SYSTEMIC CHANGE
THE PROBLEM	Famine	Underdevelopment	Exploitation
THE NEED	More food now	More development (especially rural)	More equity
VISUAL IMAGE	Starving babies	Floods, parched earth, erosion	Wealthy landowners, extravagant consumption
THE REMEDY	Relief aid	Assistance for self-help	Changes in socioeconomic systems, internally, and globally
TYPICAL BIBLE TEXTS	Good Samaritan, Joseph's granary, Matthew 25	Parable of the talents	Old Testament prophets, Luke 4, The Magnificat
TYPICAL OBJECT OF STUDY	Food deficits, population growth	Water conservancy, reforestation, infrastructure	Terms of trade, role of transnationals, land-tenure systems
CHRISTIAN VALUE	Charity, compassion	Sharing, service to neighbor	Justice, fairness, liberation
LIFESTYLE RESPONSE	Give surplus money, and food	Give money and technical aid	Support people's movements abroad, exert political pressure at home
LONG-TERM CONSEQUENCE	Dependence	Self-reliance	Shift of power and wealth from the few to the many
VARIATION ON PROVERB	"Give hungry person a fish"	"Teach hungry person how to fish"	"Let fishers have market and stop polluting their waters"

A CHRONOLOGY OF
THE CHURCHES AND HUNGER

1914. LCMS creates General Relief Board, after World War I begins.

1919. National Lutheran Council (U.S.) launches appeal for international relief.

1939. National Lutheran Council (NLC) issues emergency appeal to help Lutheran refugees in Europe and orphaned missions around the world.

1940. NLC appeal extended and given name "Lutheran World Action."

1942. LCMS establishes National Advisory Emergency Planning Council to coordinate response to war refugees.

1943. LCMS and NLC create Lutheran Commission for Prisoners of War.

1945. Lutheran World Relief (LWR) organized by NLC church bodies.

1947. Lutheran World Federation organized in Lund, Sweden.

1948. Emergency Planning Council of LCMS endorses Christian Rural Overseas Program (CROP), associated with Church World Service.

1953. LCMS General Relief Board becomes Board of World Relief; first full-time staff director named.

1953. LCMS becomes informal partner of LWR, joins as official participating church body in 1955.

1960. Lutheran Immigration Service (now Lutheran Immigration and Refugee Service) becomes joint agency of NLC and LCMS.

1965. LCMS Detroit convention adopts Mission Affirmations, including one regarding Christ's mission to the whole person.

1966. LCA Kansas City convention adopts "Poverty" social statement.

1968. ALC Omaha convention adopts "Hunger in the World" statement.

1969. LCMS Denver convention authorizes hunger committee, calls on members to give "sacrificially" for hunger alleviation.

1970. LCA Minneapolis convention adopts "World Community" social statement.

1971. LCMS Milwaukee convention asks congregations to observe annual world relief/world hunger Sunday.

1974. Bread for the World begins as a national movement of Christian citizens to lobby federal government on hunger issues.

1974. LCA Baltimore convention establishes hunger appeal for two-year period.

1974. ALC Detroit convention establishes hunger appeal for two-year period.

1975. LWR and Church World Service open joint Office on Development Policy in Washington, D.C.

1975. ALC, LCA, LCMS, and LWR hold first meeting to plan hunger education together.

1975. First national consultation of ALC farmers convened in Waverly, Iowa.

1976. Association of Evangelical Lutherans Churches is organized.

1977. Lutheran World Action is phased out.

1978. LCA opens first state advocacy office, in Harrisburg, Pennsylvania.

1984. Peak year of hunger income for ALC ($5,853,000) and AELC ($140,000).

1985. Record total income for U.S. Lutheran churches in world relief/world hunger: $20,052,000. Also highest total for LCA: $8,773,000.

1986. LCMS develops closely coordinated world relief program among Board for Mission Services, Board for Social Ministry, and LCMS World Relief.

1988. Evangelical Lutheran Church in America, uniting AELC, ALC, and LCA, begins its life.

1992. ELCA Hunger Appeal receives record income: $12,297,000.

1992-93. Year of highest LCMS World Relief income: $6,900,000.

SUGGESTIONS FOR
DISCUSSION LEADERS

Here are some ideas for leaders of groups using *Loving Neighbors Far and Near* for study in congregational settings.

1. Recruit participants for the study. Look for congregational leaders, especially those who show an interest in social ministry. Seek involvement of the congregational council. Remember to invite and involve youth.

2. Schedule four to seven 60- to 90-minute weekly sessions. (If seven, you could give one session to each chapter, combining the Introduction with Chapter One. If four, perhaps combine the Introduction with Chapter One and use subsequent sessions for Two-Three, Four-Five, and Six-Seven.) Or you might use the book as the youth/adult study content for a hunger retreat. ["Behold" (67-003184) is a packet of resources for an intergenerational hunger retreat; it is available from the ELCA Distribution Service, 800/328-4648. "Spend Yourself for the Hungry" outlines a 30-hour hunger fast for youth groups; this free resource is available from the LCMS, 800/248-1930, extension 1389.]

3. Get a copy of *Loving Neighbors Far and Near* to each participant at least two weeks before your first session. Strongly encourage participants to read the book prior to the first session.

4. Suggest that participants mark their copy as they read. They might use a *star* for information that could be shared with the congregation. An *exclamation point* could mark future actions. A *question mark* might note points where further information is needed. The marking will enrich your discussion.

5. Collect hunger resources from the congregation's library or social ministry files. Check Appendix B for organizations that can provide you with additional study helps. Put these resources on a table in the study area and suggest that participants use the resources as they prepare for your study.

6. Assign each chapter to a pair of participants. Ask them to read that chapter thoroughly and to be prepared to summarize the content at the session when that chapter will be discussed. As they have time, they might secure additional supporting information on the subject of the chapter, as well as preparing to lead the discussion of the items at the close of the chapter.

7. Assign two participants to do research on hunger in your community. How does the problem show itself? What agencies and institutions are responding? How is your congregation involved? This information might be shared at a special session or as it applies during your discussions on the book.

8. End each session with the same four questions:

a) What did we learn from this chapter that we can share with the congregation?

b) How can that information be shared?

c) What action does this chapter call us to do as individuals and as a congregation?

d) How can that action be started?

As you consider the questions, keep track of suggestions for sharing information (e.g., articles in the parish newsletter, bulletin board displays, distribution of materials) and other efforts (e.g., fund-raising activities, further education events). When possible, assign responsibility for carrying through on suggestions to specific individuals.

9. At the end of your study, ask the group to create a plan of action. What specific actions might be taken? In what order? Who might be involved? Share the plan with your social ministry or human-care committee, with the congregation council, and with the pastor.

INDEX

BIBLICAL CITATIONS

NOTES